# Matchless

## angie smith

LifeWay Press®
Nashville, Tennessee

Published by LifeWay Press® • © 2020 Angie Smith
Reprinted October 2020

ISBN 978-1-5359-5230-9 • Item 005813998

Dewey decimal classification: 232.9
Subject headings: JESUS CHRIST / CHRISTIAN LIFE / BIBLE. N.T.—
   STUDY AND TEACHING

To order additional copies of this resource, write to LifeWay Church
Resources Customer Service; One LifeWay Plaza; Nashville, TN 37234-
0113; order online at *www.lifeway.com;* fax 615.251.5933; phone toll
free 800.458.2772; or email *orderentry@lifeway.com.*

*Printed in the United States of America*

Adult Ministry Publishing • LifeWay Church Resources
One LifeWay Plaza • Nashville, TN 37234-0152

*EDITORIAL TEAM,
ADULT MINISTRY
PUBLISHING*

**Becky Loyd**
Director,
Adult Ministry

**Tina Boesch**
Manager,
Adult Ministry

**Sarah Doss**
Editorial Project Lead,
Adult Ministry Short
Term Bible Studies

**Mike Wakefield**
Content Editor

**Lindsey Bush**
**Erin Franklin**
Production Editors

**Lauren Ervin**
Graphic Designer

Dedication

For my dad, who left me his pen and told me
to use it—everything I write will be because
you told me I could, including this.

And for my (other) Audrey, who believed in
this enough for both of us and reminded
me that even the hardest pages are safe
if you know the story has a good ending.

## MEET THE AUTHOR

Angie is married to Todd Smith, lead singer of the Dove Award winning group Selah, and mom to Ellie, Abby, Kate, Audrey, and Charlotte. Angie desires to walk with Jesus authentically through the inevitable joys and sorrows of this life in a way that reflects His faithfulness to never leave us and never forsake us and to encourage other believers to do the same. This passion, along with a deep desire to understand and help others understand the Bible, has fueled her writing since 2008. She is the best-selling author of the Bible study *Seamless: Understanding the Bible as One Complete Story* as well as two children books and several books for adults including *Chasing God* and *What Women Fear*. She holds a master's degree in developmental psychology from Vanderbilt University. Angie and Todd live in Nashville with their girls, their dog, Finley, and their cat, Oliver.

# CONTENTS

# INTRODUCTION

"I am trying here to prevent anyone saying the really foolish thing that people often say about Him [that is, Christ]: 'I'm ready to accept Jesus as a great moral teacher, but I don't accept His claim to be God.' That is the one thing we must not say. A man who was merely a man and said the sort of things Jesus said would not be a great moral teacher. He would either be a lunatic—on a level with the man who says he is a poached egg—or else he would be the Devil of Hell. You must make your choice. Either this man was, and is, the Son of God: or else a madman or something worse … You can shut Him up for a fool, you can spit at Him and kill Him as a demon; or you can fall at His feet and call Him Lord and God. But let us not come up with any patronizing nonsense about His being a great human teacher. He has not left that open to us. He did not intend to."[1]

That's always been one of my favorite quotes by C. S. Lewis, and it's a perfect way to start this study. No matter who you are, you must ultimately decide what you believe to be true of Christ. Was He a real person? Was He the Son of God? The answer to these questions is either *yes* or *no*. There is no in-between. But understand, those are two very different questions.

I believe most people in the world would say Jesus was a real person who took His place among well-documented leaders and historical events. But many of those same people struggle with the fact that Jesus showed up telling folks He was the Promised One, the Messiah, the Savior. That declaration, as you can imagine, is a bit controversial. And perhaps, a bit uncomfortable.

Let me go ahead and set the tone for the rest of the study: there will most certainly be A LOT of information—maps, charts, and facts that can make you a stand-out student. Quite frankly, I would be the first one wearing a smug smile and fanning myself with an A+ paper. I love knowing details, and I'm the consummate academic. That doesn't necessarily mean I'm a scholar—it just means I'm a control freak and can't function without knowing I've fully strangled the mystery out of every possible scenario and topic. In other words, I AM FUN.

If only true faith entailed sitting in a classroom with a highlighter and eighty-seven versions of the Bible while listening to three-point sermons. Ahh. But alas, here is what I've found: that's not how this thing works.

The truth is, knowing about Jesus means nothing if you don't *know* Jesus.

And because I'm ninety-eight percent sure that one-star Janet has already left the room, I'll also confess this: that highlighted statement above makes me uncomfortable because it forces me to confront how many times I'm still prone to write only "correct" answers in blanks.

Here are a few facts:

My father was born on May 21, 1945, and he died on April 3, 2019.

He was brilliant. You would likely know some of his TV marketing campaigns. I can pretty much guarantee it. He liked to smoke good Cuban cigars every so often, and he always sat in the chair on the left side of the dinner table. His feet pointed outward when he walked, and he always dreamed he would be a published author.

When he died, he had been married to my mother for more than forty years. He loved worn-in flannel shirts and making egg sandwiches. He always greeted people with the same quickly raised hand, a tilted chin, and a smile that only showed his top teeth.

He loved when I would put my sleeping bag next to his in the backyard so he could teach me about the night sky. I never understood more than ten percent of what he was saying, but I loved to listen to him.

He pinched his nose and tossed his head back when he was laughing his biggest laughs, and he called me "kid" for my entire life.

Of all the titles I've held in my life, "Dane's kid" was the one I was most proud of.

I could fill pages with this kind of information.

But here's the truth—you will never smell his cigars or hear his laughter. You can't know what it's like to settle into the nook of his chest when you're crying or smell the old leather seats in the 1957 MGA we restored together. You can listen to me tell you everything you need to know in order to sketch an image, but you would never be able to paint it with all the nuances of color and shade.

When I think of my dad, I don't recall facts; those are available to everyone. What no one else will ever know is the way it felt to be loved by him for forty-three years. It's the colors that make the art mine.

And when it comes to Jesus, most of us can't start there, can we? The facts are familiar but the intimacy is not.

His story has been told and retold for hundreds of years, but I can't help but wonder if you've missed the part that makes it come to life. The part where He tells you what He has known before time began. The beautiful, impossible, unavoidable, life-shaking truth that drips color and life onto black and white pages.

*You, kid …*

*Yes, you. You aren't just an observer.*

In fact, He has painted the nuanced colors of your life onto the canvas, and I wonder, *Have you seen it there?*

I know. I have a hard time with it too. But a wise man once taught me this simple lesson: I don't have to understand the way the stars shift in order to love the voice of the teacher.

So join me on this eight-session adventure as we learn the ways and wonders of our matchless Savior. We may not be able to answer all the questions or fill in all the blanks, but we'll see the colors of His story and, in His story, find our own.

*Angie*

one

WEEK 1

# PAST: LOOKING BACK, LOOKING FORWARD

It would be easy (ish) to write a study that told you all of the facts of Jesus' life. I mean, there were a whole lot of cool details like raising people from the dead and calming a wild sea.

We're going to learn a lot of those stories, but I want to say this before we start: we aren't going to get to all of them. I know. I know. You bought this little book thinking it would explain every single miracle and teaching of Christ. Which means there's good news and bad news. The bad news is that we aren't going to cover it all. The good news is that you're an optimist, and I like that.

My hope is that you'll walk away with a sense of who Jesus was and what He did, but in my experience there's nothing in black and white that can convince you that there is color. God painted all of these amazing stories onto pages, and He hasn't put down His brush. Scripture is alive and active, and we get to be a part of it.

We don't fall in love with Him because we know the story of His life; we fall in love with Him when we realize that our names are written in the gaps of white between the print.

You'll notice there are several days of homework coming up that don't seem like they're related to Jesus, but I promise they are. Well, all of them except the week that's completely focused on the evolution of fashion and hairstyles in the Old Testament. Even though I had trouble making a solid link, it just felt right.

You may know the first three words in the Bible, "In the beginning …"

Let's head to Genesis (the first book in the Old Testament). I mean, the very beginning is always the best place to start, don't you think?

I'm so honored that you're here. I have a feeling we're going to be great friends by the end of this adventure.

## GROUP SESSION GUIDE

Rather than a formal leader guide in the back, we've provided what we hope is a simple and functional group plan on these pages. Each week will begin with an introductory page like the previous one. Then you'll find a two-page group guide like this. My suggestion is that you divide your group time into three parts.

1. After this first week, you'll first discuss the previous week's personal study.
2. Then watch the video segment so I can come along. After all, you wouldn't want to leave me out, would you? Where's the fun in that?
3. Finally, end your group time with a closing discussion of the video. (And of course I'd recommend a party, but that's just me.)

The session guide for this first meeting is for us to get to know each other. Then we'll each go do our personal study. (It will be fun, I promise.) Each day, plan to spend a few minutes with that day's study. Don't worry if some days you don't get it all. This isn't a race, and you can come back later. When we meet next group session, we'll have this week's study to discuss. Now let's get to know each other, and I'll join you by way of video.

## SESSION 1: INTRODUCTION

Getting to know each other:

> \* *What's one thing you want your group to know about you?*

> \* *What drew you to this study?*

**WATCH SESSION 1 (VIDEO RUN TIME 11:22)**

## DISCUSS

> \* *What part of the video spoke to you the most? Why?*

* How did Angie's honesty about her doubts surrounding Jesus resonate with you? What have been your own doubts in coming to Jesus?

* What do you hope to gain as you study and participate with this group in the coming weeks?

* Angie says, "The hard things are going to happen anyway; and I'd rather go through them with the right person." How does that sit with you? What does it make you think of from your past? What does it make you hope for your future with your community? With Jesus?

* How about you? Who is Jesus to you? What first comes to mind when you hear His name?

* What would it look like for you to "paint your faith" as Angie says in the video, instead of just going through the motions?

Video sessions available for purchase or rent
at *LifeWay.com/Matchless*

DAY 1

# IN THE GARDEN

Question: Where are you?

Hey! And now the adventure begins! Let's get down to business and learn all about the Pentateuch.

The what?

Glad you asked. The best part of writing a Bible study is getting to assume you're answering my questions exactly the way I want you to. Which, naturally, is the correct way. The Pentateuch is simply the first five books of the Bible.

*Why don't you go ahead and write them down, and then we'll get into some more background and detail.*

Perfect. Now let me explain why I want to start with these particular books of the Bible. In case you didn't know, the Bible is comprised of two sections: the Old Testament and the New Testament. The Old Testament covers history before Christ's birth, and the New Testament covers the life of Christ and beyond.

Back to the Torah. Oh wait, didn't mention that yet. The Pentateuch can also be called the Torah, the Law, or the books of Moses.

*Who wrote them? (There might be a clue in the previous statement.)*

Now let's get down to some serious talk. These five books are the heart of the Jewish faith. The Jews are God's chosen people—unique and favored by Him. The Old Testament is basically the story of God lovingly pursuing His people while they reject Him over and over.

Hang tight for a few minutes if you already know this information. Realize that a lot of people don't, and it's super important to understand the whole story. I'm going to give you the really basic framework, and we'll fill it in as we move along in the study.

The first five books of the Bible (along with the rest of the Old Testament) point to a Savior who will come to rescue His people. Christians believe that Jesus Christ is that Savior, but Jewish people disagree and are still waiting for their Messiah to come. So basically, Christians and Jews both recognize and accept the Old Testament, but only Christians believe in the New Testament. What we'll be doing in this study is making connections between the Old and New Testaments to help you see how Jesus fulfilled all the prophecies about His coming that were made in the Old Testament. Does that make sense? I hope so. And now I will digress for a paragraph or so because I want you to feel welcome in my world.

I went to a lot of Bar and Bat Mitzvah's in my "how are your bangs defying gravity?" phase of life. I have now fallen head-first into a suppressed memory that involves a store called Chatterlings, where I convinced my dad to buy me a dress that was unfortunate in design and fit. It had black silk ruching on the bodice and a blue taffeta skirt that involved a lot of netting. Pouf sleeves? Of course. Blue and covered in tiny black velvet hearts? Yes, because WHY WOULDN'T THEY BE?

God bless the little Angela who truly believed the dress would be the tipping point in her quest for Josh's love. I was one slow dance away from eternal bliss. Alas, 'twas not to be. I'm sure he looks back with regret.

Sorry. Let's get back to the Bible. First up? Genesis.

The first part of the Book of Genesis tells how God created the world and two people named Adam and Eve. Keep in mind we're looking at the Bible from a bird's-eye view for now (partly because I used up a lot of my word count on taffeta).

God gives Adam and Eve the perfect world. No shame, sadness, or sin. It's paradise in every sense of the word, just as God desired. But it doesn't stay that way for long because Satan was determined to separate Adam and Eve from their loving God.

Sidenote: Satan is God's enemy as well as ours. He was once one of God's angels, but because he wanted to be God's equal, he was cast out of heaven, along with other angels who rebelled with him (Rev. 12:7-9). Is he still real? He is. There is a war being waged between good and evil that we can't see, and it affects every moment of our lives. We'll come back to this in a bit, but basically Satan's entire existence revolves around wreaking havoc on God's creation.

*Go ahead and read Genesis 3:1-7. Describe what happens.*

**PROPHECY**

Prediction, instruction, or encouragement that God (through the Holy Spirit) gave to a human prophet[1]

**BAR MITZVAH**

Coming of age ceremony for Jewish boys (age thirteen)

**BAT MITZVAH**

Coming of age ceremony for Jewish girls (age twelve)[2]

This incident is referred to as "The fall," and it's basically the story of how sin entered the world.

Let's pause for a moment. I don't want to miss any opportunities to fill in blanks you might have in your mind. In case you just see the word sin and it registers as "doing something bad," let me take a second to explain it. Sin is much worse than your average mistake. A better definition—sin is *doing, thinking, or speaking things that aren't in line with the moral character of God or refusing to do the things that would honor Him*. Even that definition doesn't capture the weight of offense, but we have to start somewhere. And trust me, we're going to go a lot further with this sin problem.

Bad choices can sure turn things upside down, can't they?

God gave Adam and Eve everything they could ever want. The perfect garden. The perfect world. The perfect life. All of it. And He only had one rule.

* *Read Genesis 2:16-17. What does He tell them not to do?*

God made it pretty clear, didn't He? Don't eat the fruit from a particular tree in the perfect garden. One tree. *One*, Eve.

* *Review what took place in Genesis 3:1-7.*

Notice that Satan never insisted. He never forced. He used the most powerful method of connecting to other people: *He asked a question.*

*Why wouldn't He want you to have every good thing? Surely you can bend the rules. If He's for you, then He would want this! But ... is He?*

It's so subtle. He isn't stupid.

* *Once their eyes are opened, what do they do (3:7-8)?*

Turns out that using a couple of fig leaves and ducking under trees isn't an effective strategy for hiding from the God of the universe. (But can we at least acknowledge their industriousness in the midst of a crisis? A for effort, folks.)

I'm making a lot of promises about this study, aren't I? This isn't a ploy for you to keep up with your homework. But if you don't, you might be completely lost and confused for the rest of your natural life. Your choice.

SOME OTHER NAMES FOR SATAN IN THE BIBLE:

* devil * tempter
* liar and father of lies
* evil one * enemy
* accuser * god of this age

\* *What does God ask Adam and Eve in Genesis 3:9?*

For the record, that is God's first recorded question: "Where are you?"

As a bit of clarification, the God of the universe has not lost His first two people. He isn't fretting and kicking Himself for not keeping track of them.

He is asking a question that will forevermore be posed alongside the question Satan asked. God's question has nothing to do with their physical location.

*He wants to know the position of their hearts toward Him.*

Satan asked: *Are you sure?*

God asked: *Where are you?*

I want to take a second and let you answer those questions.

I can't help but ask if you're confused at this point, thinking you had signed up for a study about Jesus but instead you got fig loincloths. If that's the case, I am SO happy you are here. Hang in there with me. I promise it'll all come together in a little while. It's just that it's such an amazing story, and I don't want you to miss it.

\* *In what areas of your life right now do you wonder if God is really for you and if He has your best in mind?*

\* *Describe the way you would answer God's question—where are you in terms of trusting and believing in Him?*

If your answers are anything like mine, they show you've got some struggles with wholeheartedly believing God without at least hearing a bit of Satan's voice. I think that's normal. As children of God, we are prime targets for the enemy. We're a threat to Satan, and he's not going down without a fight.

After Adam and Eve defied God, He issued a curse that we still live under. I'm not going into detail about the curse right this minute, but I will say it's the reason I've had five epidurals and threatened the life of an intern who likely chose another profession shortly after our interaction.

I know this isn't the happiest start to a Bible study, but we got through it. Tomorrow is going to be better(ish).

Onward!

DAY 2
# ABRAHAM, ISAAC, AND JACOB

Let's look at a couple other major players in Genesis.

*Flip over to Genesis 12 and read verses 1-3.*

*Who is the Lord talking to?*

*Where is He telling him to go?*

*What does God promise Abram in verses 2-3?*

*What phrase indicates you and I are part of that promise?*

These are some of the most important words in all of the Old Testament. Without processing them, you can't understand the New Testament. It's that big of a deal.

Here's a quick summary of what happened next: God tells Abram that the blessing will come through a son (Gen. 15:1-6). That all sounded well and good except for the fact that Sarai is barren and as old as dirt. Time passes but still no son is born. So Sarai, who was obviously still both (1) barren and (2) older than previously-mentioned dirt, decides God might need some help with His plan. She comes up with a clever workaround.

*Read Genesis 16:1-5 and summarize what happens with the plan.*

Because Sarai's maidservant Hagar belongs to her, any child Hagar has would be considered Sarai's, so Sarai tells Abram to make it happen.

I'd be lying if I said this plan was on my top ten list for solving this particular problem.

Anyway, Abram begrudgingly—hmm, I actually couldn't find that part in the Bible—gets Hagar pregnant, and they name their son Ishmael.

But wait, there's more.

Turns out Sarah and Abraham do have a baby son years later, and they name him Isaac. (In Gen. 17, God changes their names to Sarah and Abraham.) After Isaac was born, there was really no need for Hagar and her kid to hang around anymore, so Sarah makes Abraham kick them out. Y'all, *Lifetime* has nothing on some good Old Testament stories.

*Read Genesis 17:17-22. Describe the promise God makes to Abraham before Isaac is conceived.*

God tells Abraham the covenant will come through his son Isaac, not Ishmael, because Isaac is the child of the promise (Gal. 4:21-23). This story of the two sons is definitely more interesting and applicable when you know this tidbit about the two brothers:

*Ishmael is the father of the Arabs, and Isaac is the father of the Jews.*

Read that again and really let it soak in. Some of the news you might watch tonight has its roots in these half-brothers. Isn't that crazy?

These are real people and stories, y'all.

I know it will take you a few minutes, but there's a story of significance in the Abraham/Isaac saga that I don't want you to miss.

*Read Genesis 22:1-18. What does God ask Abraham to do and why?*

*How is the work of Jesus foreshadowed in this story?*

God puts Abraham to the test and asks him to sacrifice his only son.

*Go and sacrifice your only son? What?*

## NAME CHANGE

*Abram*

Meaning "father is exalted"

*Abraham*

Meaning "father of a multitude"

*Sarai*

Meaning "princess"

*Sarah*

Variant form of "Sarai," meaning "princess"

I can't imagine what that must have felt like, but I do know that Abraham was a man of faith, so he set off with Isaac. When they get to the top of the mountain, Abraham lays Isaac on the altar in obedience, fully aware that he is about to have to kill him. Just as Abraham raises his knife, God stops him and tells him it isn't necessary; God provides a sacrifice for him. This will mean more to you as we get further ahead, but just remember the part where God provides a ram as a sacrifice in place of Isaac. It's a foreshadowing of what's to come. (Spoiler alert: It involves Jesus.)

It's a story that will echo through the centuries, all the way to a hill outside Jerusalem where the sacrifice of an only Son would take place.

Let's keep going with Abraham's story. When he is somewhere around the ripe old age of 140, he decides it's time to find Isaac a wife. Abraham doesn't want his son to marry a Canaanite woman, so he sends his best servant back to Abraham's homeland to find one. The servant set off, asking God to show him who Isaac's wife was supposed to be. It was obviously the hand of God that led him to find her, because it turned out that she was (wait for it ... ) Isaac's cousin, Rebekah. Just so you know, marrying your cousin wasn't an unusual practice at the time. Keep it all in the family, y'all.

Rebekah's brother Laban approves of the marriage and sends her to be with Isaac, who falls in love with her immediately. Because family ties run strong.

Rebekah gets pregnant and realizes she is having twins. (I've been there. Fortunately, our stories diverged at that point.) They are wrestling in her womb, so she asks God why this is happening, and she got FUN NEWS.

*Read Genesis 25:22-23. What does the Lord tell her about her twins?

When she delivers the boys, Esau (the oldest) is covered in red hair that's described as looking like a cloak. I'm sure he loved that coming up at every family get-together. Jacob is born next, holding Esau's foot in an effort to be the firstborn.

I'm skipping over some details, but you need to know that the prophecy about the twins comes true. When they are older, Jacob pulls a fast one on Esau and steals Esau's birthright. Then with the help of his mom, Jacob tricks his father Isaac into giving him the blessing that is supposed

---

This icon marks when a story or passage in the Old Testament clearly points to Jesus.

JESUS

Why wouldn't Abraham want Isaac to marry a woman from Canaan, the land they lived in?

The people in Canaan didn't follow God, so looking for Isaac's wife in Abraham's homeland gave them a better chance to find someone who believed the same as Abe's family did.

to be given to Esau. It's a long story, but let's just say it involves his mother gluing some red goat hair on his arms (it's the gift that keeps on giving), dressing him in his brother's clothes, and telling him to go into his dad's room (who was blind and half-dead) to convince him he is Esau. As if there was ever another option, right? Well, it turns out, her trick works, which leads to Esau serving Jacob instead of vice versa.

As you can imagine, Esau is less than pleased when he finds out. In fact, he vows to kill his brother over it. When Rebekah gets wind of Esau's rage, she helps Jacob get out of town. She convinces Isaac to send Jacob away to find a wife, so off Jacob goes to the land of Laban. While he's on the road, Jacob has a dream and is promised something that might sound familiar.

> BIRTHRIGHT
> AND BLESSING
> *Birthright*: special privileges for the firstborn male child in the family, including a double portion of the inheritance and receiving the father's major blessing[3]

\* *Read Genesis 28:13-15 and write down what God tells him.*

\* *Let's do a quick breakdown of where the blessing has traveled.*

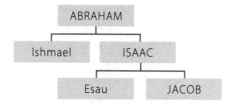

Alright, keep those names in mind. In fact, go ahead and memorize them; they're going to show up *all* the way to the end of the story.

And here's when the plot twist happens: the trickster gets tricked.

Jacob falls in love with a woman named Rachel and works for her dad, Laban, for seven years in order to marry her. Remember, Laban is Rebekah's brother, so yes, we have another cousin marriage in the works. I'm guessing their family reunions were super confusing. Hey, Uncle-um-cousin Bob! Good to see you, pal!

Here's where it takes a turn. Rachel has an older sister named Leah.

\* *Read Genesis 29:17 and note how both sisters are described.*

To be honest, scholars aren't sure what Leah's weak-eyed description means. But because it's compared with Rachel being "beautiful in form and appearance," we're assuming it's not a compliment. (And besides that, Leah's name also means "wild cow."⁴ No joke.) Bless her heart. The problem is that the oldest daughter is supposed to be married before the younger. So Laban decides to pull a little switcheroo. Instead of Rachel, Laban gives Leah to Jacob. Evidently, Jacob parties hard on his wedding night because he doesn't realize what has happened until the next morning.

I have a lot of questions about this whole situation.

Jacob isn't happy (and I'm guessing Rachel isn't either—like, where is she hanging out during all of this? Didn't anyone notice that she is MIA?). But after the week-long wedding reception, Laban allows Rachel to marry Jacob right away as long as he promises to stay and work for him another seven years. As you can imagine, this whole situation is *unpleasant*—especially after Jacob makes it clear that Rachel is his favorite. It really ramps up after Leah starts having babies and Rachel can't get pregnant. They both come up with some work-around plans. Take a stab at who they might bring into the picture to have a lot of kids. Yeah, their slave girls. A baby-making war ensues. Final count: Rachel has two sons, while Leah has six sons and one daughter. (Both of their slave girls have two sons apiece.)

JACOB

Leah
— Reuben
— Simeon
— Levi
— Judah
— Issachar
— Zebulun

Zilpah
— Gad
— Asher

Bilhah
— Dan
— Naphtali

Rachel
— Joseph
— Benjamin

* *Whose sons do you think became Jacob's favorites?*

Oh, Leah, don't worry. Your name will forever be tied to the most important story ever written.

All of Jacob's kids are born while he is still living in Haran (the place he fled to get away from Esau). But after being there twenty years, God tells Jacob it's time to go home. Remember, when Jacob left home he was on the run from Esau, and he is nervous he might still be looking for revenge. As Jacob and his entourage travel back, he finds out that Esau and an army of four hundred men are closing in on him. And they aren't carrying streamers and balloons, either. Jacob is terrified and ends up alone the night before confronting Esau, and he has a life-altering experience.

&ast;Read Genesis 32:24-30. Who does Jacob wrestle?

&ast;What does he insist he must have before he stops wrestling?

&ast;What does God ask him in verse 27?

God wants Jacob to say his own name because it has always been associated with deception and cheating. Again—He isn't in heaven like, "Sorry … what was it? Joshua? No. But it's something with a 'J,' right?"

&ast;God calls Jacob by that name, and then what does He do?

**JACOB**

Means "he grasps the heel" or "he cheats, supplants"

Jacob is no longer the same man; he has been given a new name and a new reputation. He will be called Israel from now on—the name given to him by God.

**ISRAEL**

Means "he strives against God"

&ast;Look at the last family tree we did. How many sons did Jacob have?

And these, my friends, are the twelve tribes of Israel. (Why? Because their dad is now named Israel.)

Don't worry if you don't know what the twelve tribes are—you will.

Hey, before you tap out for today, go back and look at your work. You have no idea how much more beautiful these names will be in just a little bit. Get your goat hair scented candle ready, and we'll meet back here tomorrow.

Israelites, Hebrews, and Jews are all names used in the Bible to refer to the same group, God's Old Testament chosen people.

DAY 3

# TWO DELIVERERS: JOSEPH & MOSES

Oh, sweet Jacob. We get it. You love Rachel more than Leah. And now you're choosing one son over the other? What is with you having favorites? This isn't gonna end well. Well, actually it is, but it won't be for a little while.

I'm ahead of myself just a bit.

When we last saw Jacob he was wrestling God and getting a new name. He also knew he was about to run into his brother Esau, who was probably still not super pumped to see him. Good news: it turns out to be a great reunion. It was actually a pretty profound picture of forgiveness, and that's a theme we're going to see a lot as we keep going.

If you want to read more about the Jacob-Esau reunion, go to Genesis 33.

Once Jacob and his family get back to Canaan, the "favorite" problem shows up again.

> \* Read Genesis 37:1-4. What does Jacob do to show his favoritism to one son?

Jacob really wants to make his pride in Joseph clear, which is why he decides to give his favorite son a lil' gift. He makes Joseph a coat, which can only be described as a "statement piece." Now, we're not exactly sure what makes this coat so special. It might have been multi-colored[5]or long-sleeved, but whatever it is, it isn't subtle. Once Joseph starts strutting around in the cloak, it's pretty obvious he is daddy's favorite.

> \* As you can imagine, Joseph's brothers aren't pleased. In fact, how do they feel about him (v. 4)?

I may be the only one, but I used to think Bible passages were intimidating. I'd read them and think, *There's no way I'd ever be able to understand because the terminology would have been too hard.*

*OK, sweet sister, I want you to see what I'm talking about. Go to Genesis 37:3-4. Do you have a little more context now?*

If you happen to feel like Bible stories slip through your hands when you try to read them on your own, I want you to hear me say this LOUD AND CLEAR: you are the exact target audience God had in mind.

*You.* You have everything you need to figure all of this stuff out on your own, but I'm grateful you bought this study anyway because I have a lot of kids who I want to send to college.

*Read verses 5-11 and summarize the parts you understand. Just tell the general story in really basic terms.*

*Write down words or ideas that were new or confusing to you.*

The summary you gave was probably getting at the heart of the story. At some point, Joseph would rule over his brothers. As for how he would rise to that position and why, you'll have to keep reading. Always leave the audience on the edge of a cliff. That's the writer's job.

I'm guessing that whatever you wrote for the second question deals more with the details. *What does it mean to be "binding sheaves"? Who are the eleven stars bowing down?*

Take these words to heart: you don't have to understand every detail to understand the main ideas of the story. Don't let the details keep you from reading Scripture. Instead, let them draw you in. "Don't get stuck on the sheaves." I plan to make that a T-shirt because COLLEGE AND ALL.

I bet you're further along than you think you are. Look how you just summarized that story! God helps us understand the Bible through His Spirit. More on that later (*cliff), but for now, it's important for you to know you're not alone. You don't need to understand every law in Leviticus or prophecy in Revelation. Right this second you don't need to be stressed if you don't even know what Leviticus and Revelation are. I genuinely believe we're so intimidated by these kinds of things that we just pull back and believe it's above our heads. One thing our enemy loves to do is make us feel like we can't understand the Bible, but it's not true.

Moving on to the section we'll call, "Why Jacob's family counselor has job security," we are going to read about the brothers getting really annoyed at "Mr. Statement Piece." And they don't use the emotional tools they've paid so much to learn. Instead, they concoct a plan to kill him but then decide to throw him in a well. AS YOU DO. But then they change their minds, pull him out, and sell him to some traders—bottom-line, he ends up as a slave in Egypt.

*Read Genesis 37:31-35. How do the brothers try to cover their crime? What is Jacob's reaction?*

But don't worry, the brothers have a plan to cover their tracks. They drag his coat through goat's blood and tell their dad that Joseph must have been eaten by a wild animal. AS YOU DO. Jacob thinks he's lost his favorite son. What he doesn't know is that Joseph is not only alive, but he will rise to power and will eventually be the second most important man in Egypt: Pharaoh's right-hand man. On his way to the top, Joseph has to deal with his boss's desperate housewife and a stint in prison.

*Read Genesis 39:1-4,21-23. What's the key phrase here?*

Regardless of what Joseph goes through, the Lord is with Him. And eventually, the gift God has given him to interpret dreams will pave the way for him to be Pharaoh's second-in-command.

The dream interpretation thing really comes in handy when Pharaoh dreams about Egypt's upcoming famine. He tells Pharaoh that there will be seven years of feast followed by seven years of famine. As a result, Joseph makes sure Egypt is well-stocked with grain to prepare for the future.

The famine makes its way to Canaan where Joseph's father and brothers are still living. They need food, and the only place to get it is Egypt. Little did they know, Joey will be calling the shots. When they finally come face-to-face with Joseph, they don't recognize him. But he knows exactly who they are.

*Read Genesis 45:1-15 and describe what happens once they get there.*

*How does Joseph view what his brothers have done (vv. 7-8; 50:19-20)?*

Joseph is primed for payback, but instead he chooses forgiveness. See, I told you we'd keep seeing that! I would never lie to you. Or throw you in a well.

After Joseph tells his brothers he is over the fact that goat's blood doesn't wash out of coats, they decide to move to Egypt. Yay for grain! Things are looking up. But, as you may have guessed, they don't stay that way.

*Read Exodus 1:6-14 and describe what happens.*

Hundreds of years later, a new Pharaoh realizes that this rapidly multiplying group of Israelites might actually become a threat to Egypt. So Pharaoh makes them slaves and insists that all baby boys born to the Israelites must be drowned at birth.

But, there is one baby boy whose mother hides him for as long as she can and then sets him in a basket and pushes him into the water. AS YOU DO. She prays for his safety, and in an ironic turn of events, the baby is discovered by Pharaoh's daughter, who names him Moses and raises him as an Egyptian.

What we have to remember about this situation is that Moses is born a Hebrew. You can understand why he decides to kill an Egyptian beating an Israelite. He buries the body and somehow presumes he can waltz right back into his normal life without anyone knowing about it. Turns out that's not the case. Once he realizes his secret is out, he flees the country and winds up tending sheep in the desert where he assumes no one will be able to find him.

*Read Exodus 3:1-10. Who finds Moses, and what does He want?*

At this point, God's people have been in slavery for more than four hundred years, and it is time for them to be delivered. God chooses Moses to lead them. Moses reluctantly accepts the call and ends up back

## HOW DO WE SEE JESUS IN JOSEPH'S STORY?

Joseph as deliverer points to Jesus as our ultimate Deliverer.

Deliverance is a pretty clear theme we see throughout the entire Bible.

in the court of Pharaoh—this time to insist that the Egyptian leader let God's people go.

I mean, how cool is it that God has Moses stand in front of Pharaoh to say these powerful words? (You may recognize them.) "Let my people go" (Ex. 5:1).

Pharaoh refuses, so God sends ten plagues to show Pharaoh He means business. The first nine plagues make no difference; Pharaoh's heart is hardened, and he remains steadfast in his decisions.

You guys. I'm so excited to be on this journey with you. It's kind of awkward timing for me to say this because we're talking about plagues and all, but we're about to walk into something amazing.

Turns out the last plague is the worst: if Pharaoh refuses again, God will kill every firstborn child in Egypt. And here we go.

## THE PLAGUES

**#1 Water to blood**
*Exodus 7:14-25*

**#2 Frogs**
*Exodus 8:1-15*

**#3 Gnats**
*Exodus 8:16-19*

**#4 Flies**
*Exodus 8:20-32*

**#5 Death of Livestock**
*Exodus 9:1-7*

**#6 Boils**
*Exodus 9:8-12*

**#7 Hail**
*Exodus 9:13-35*

**#8 Locusts**
*Exodus 10:1-20*

**#9 Darkness**
*Exodus 10:21-29*

**#10 Death of Firstborn**
*Exodus 11; 12:29-32*

* *Read Exodus 12:1-7. What is each family supposed to get? On which day does that happen?*

* *Starting in verse 5, we're going to do your favorite thing. It's pretty long but that's because this is one of the most amazing parts of Scripture.*

*⁵Your _____ shall be without _____, a male a _____ old. You may take it from the sheep or from the goats, ⁶and you shall keep it until the _____th day of this month, when the whole assembly of the congregation of ___ shall _____ their _____ at _____. ⁷Then they shall take some of the _____ and put it on the two _____ and the _____ of the _____ in which they eat it.*

* *Now read Exodus 12:11-13.*

God would pass over all of the houses that had the blood of a lamb on them, because those were His people. Pass. Over. Do you get it?

It's the first PASSOVER because He *passed over* them! I love it. And just wait for tomorrow where we'll be hanging out with Moses in the wilderness. AS YOU DO. If you're looking for an inspirational candle, I'd suggest "beachy."

DAY 4

# JOURNEY TO THE PROMISED LAND

We're going to pick up exactly where we left off and see what happens to Moses and the Israelites. Go ahead and light your blue candle. Yeah, I know the scent/color code rules.

So they've left Egypt, and things are going swimmingly as the Israelites head toward the promised land. That is, until they discovered that they would have to swim to get there. They get to the Red Sea and realize that there's a fine line between Siri saying, "you're driving a car" and "you're riding on a barge." We've all been there, right?

＊*Read Exodus 13:17–14:4. How does God lead the people?*

＊*Why does He take them on this path to the Red Sea?*

God is obviously guiding, providing for, and protecting His people. I mean, He splits the Red Sea so they can flee from the Egyptians and continue their trek to the land He has promised them. Read that again. HE SPLITS THE SEA. When they get thirsty, God provides water from a rock. When they get hungry, God provides manna (bread) by dropping it from the sky. Are they filled with gratitude? Nope. They grumble. A lot. They get bored with the food selection and tired of walking. Some of them even say they would rather be in Egypt again. Awesome. I know how much that must have really blessed the God who just brought them out of slavery.

＊*A few critically important events occur in this next little bit of the Old Testament. Open your Bibles to Exodus 20 and write down what God says in verses 1-2. (Yes, God. Not Moses. This is business, folks).*

## THE TEN COMMANDMENTS

1. "You shall have no other gods before me."
2. "You shall not make for yourself a carved image."
3. "You shall not take the name of the Lord your God in vain."
4. "Remember the Sabbath day, to keep it holy."
5. "Honor your father and your mother."
6. "You shall not murder."
7. "You shall not commit adultery."
8. "You shall not steal."
9. "You shall not bear false witness against your neighbor."
10. "You shall not covet ... anything that is your neighbor's."

*What tone do verses 3-4 set for this list of commands?*

God establishes His authority and makes it unequivocally clear that He is to be first in their lives. Then He finishes out the list of rules that are the most important for them to keep, which we know as the Ten Commandments.

Later on it's going to be really important for you to know what the term "The Law" means, so let's just take a second to cover it.

The Ten Commandments, while being the most essential, are far from the only laws that were given to the people. They are foundational to knowing who God is and what He requires from His people. But I'm just going to tell you, there are *chapters* of the Old Testament filled with laws. Laws. Laws. *Laws!*

Like, "If you touch a chicken between 4-6 p.m. on the first Sunday of the month, you can't look anyone in the eye until 5:15 on Wednesday."

Well, that's not an actual law, but it's not necessarily more extreme than some of the real ones. Seriously.

*Read the following passages and write out the law recorded there:*

*Exodus 21:17*

*Exodus 22:3*

*Exodus 23:19*

So kids, you might want to watch your mouth. Take it easy on a thief if he breaks in at night. And make sure to cook your young goat in chicken broth.

While these and other laws may sound a little strange, God gives them to His people to help them.

*Read Exodus 24:3. How do the people respond to all the commands from God?*

The Israelites tell God they will keep all of the laws, all of the time.

Spoiler alert: That doesn't happen. Mostly because it's impossible. For them and for us.

Not to get ahead of myself, but just know one of the best things the Law does is show us our need for Jesus.

After God gives them the laws, He tells Moses to build something.

＊Read Exodus 25:8-9. What is God asking Moses to make?

＊Why?

CUBIT

*A first century unit of measure—around eighteen inches, typically the distance from a person's elbow to the tip of their middle finger[6]*

In the next few chapters, God will give *very* specific instructions on how to build this tabernacle. Like, down to the cubits. You are more than welcome to study and memorize the layout God gives Moses, and then read on to see if they built it exactly to God's specs. Or I can just tell you that they did.

So as they are heading toward the promised land, they now carry a portable tent they can bring from place to place. Inside it is the most sacred object in their lives: the ark of the covenant.

There are three things inside the ark of the covenant: the Ten Commandments, a jar filled with manna (to remind them of how God provided for them in the desert), and a staff that belonged to a fellow named Aaron. We don't have a lot of time to talk about Aaron, but he was Moses' brother.

＊Read Exodus 26:31-33. Where is the ark to be placed?

＊What is the purpose of the curtain?

(I really, really, really hope those last couple of questions aren't that familiar to you, because if that's the case, you're going to love where this whole thing ends up.)

There are different sections in the tabernacle (just a name for the tent that covered all the stuff). The most important area in the tabernacle was called the "Most Holy Place," where the ark of the covenant was located (Ex. 26:34; it is also referred to as the "holy of holies"). God's presence resided in this sacred place where only the high priest could enter, and he could only do so once a year—on the Day of Atonement. The Israelites believed the Spirit of God existed behind a veil they could not pass; in fact, they thought they would be struck dead if they did.

Got it? Good.

Now we need to fast-forward a bit.

On the way to take over Canaan, the Israelites ran into a little problem of their own making. After a group of twelve spies comes back from a reconnaissance mission into the new land, ten of them give a negative report, saying the inhabitants of the land are too big and scary for them to take on. Only Joshua and Caleb say they should move forward. Unfortunately, the people choose to believe the majority report and turned into a wild mob (Num. 13–14). To summarize: They don't exactly follow through with the plan God gave them—not even close.

> * Read Deuteronomy 1:34-40. What was their punishment as a result of their disobedience?

> * Which group of people gets to see the promised land?

> * In verse 40, what does God tell the people to do?

So they are sent into the desert for forty (the number that always indicates testing in the Bible) years.[8] When the unbelieving generation dies out, the new crew takes a second shot at entering the promised land.

### DAY OF ATONEMENT

*The one day of the year the high priest entered the most holy place in the temple to give an offering for the sins of the entire nation (Lev. 16:16-28)[7]*

\* Read Deuteronomy 31:1-3; 34:1-12. Who becomes the new leader, and what happens to Moses?

Moses never sets foot in the promised land because he had disobeyed God's instructions at one point in the journey (Num. 20:1-13), but God does allow him to see the land from a mountaintop. Soon after, Moses dies, although no one knows exactly where his body is (it's somewhere in the land of Moab) because God Himself buried him.

After Moses' death, Joshua leads the people into the new land where they win their first major battle.

\* What's the name of the place they conquered (Josh. 6:2)?

And now I'm singing the song. If you know, you know.

So they moved into the new land, and they all lived happily ever after. Well, not quite. In fact, it didn't really go all that well for the Israelites. The gist of the story is that they consistently disobey God and fall into sin—worshiping false gods, intermarrying with the pagan people who lived in the land, and basically turning their backs on God. God had warned them that if they did this, He would judge them and remove His hand of protection from them. Which is exactly what happened. The cycle repeats itself time after time. They are defeated by their enemies. Then they apologize and promise they will never do it again, until they do it again.

During this time period, three groups of people led the people. First, we have the judges (because, um, they were judges). The next group was called kings (because they were—you guessed it—kings). And then finally we have the prophets (yep, same). We'll talk more about all these folks tomorrow.

Speaking of tomorrow—it'll be our last day hanging out in the Old Testament, and then we'll be good and ready to move on to the New Testament. You've got this.

DAY 5

# PROPHETS, JUDGES, KINGS, & THE COMING KING

Last day of the Old Testament, y'all. And it's a doozy. Jam-packed with near-death experiences, a harp player who kills a giant, a major geographical shift, and the construction of a very special building.

As you can tell, there's a lot happening in this section of Scripture, so we're just going to do a drive-by of the things that will matter the most as we move ahead.

Let's start with a little review. Ready?

\* *Who led the Jews out of Egypt?*

\* *What happened the first time they considered entering the promised land, after the spies gave their report?*

   *They _____ _____ _____ _____ for _____ years.*

\* *What did the people build to bring the presence of God with them as they traveled?*

\* *Who led the people into Canaan when they actually made it there?*

\* *Bonus points if you can remember the three things contained in the ark of the covenant.*

   1.

   2.

   3.

Well done.

So the Israelites *finally* move into Canaan. And, get this: God tells them to get rid of the people who have been living there. *Get rid of.* As in ... kill them.

Shockingly, the Israelites don't listen to God and decide it would be fine to leave the Canaanites happily living in the land. I'm sure they figure there will be enough milk and honey to go around. Coexist, you guys. No way that could go wrong.

But, what they don't understand is that letting the Canaanites be next door will lead them away from God. They start picking up some bad habits from their neighbors and try to chart their own course.

God sends a bunch of people (think foreign armies) to try to get the Israelites in-line and warn them about what is going to happen if they keep going their own way.

So they cry uncle and ask God for help. This is when God sends some folks called judges (ten points if you remember why they're called that) to try to get them back on track spiritually. So the Israelites turn things around.

Until they don't.

And they fall back into the old patterns of sin. We see the same cycle of sin and defeat here that we talked about yesterday. Frankly, it gets a bit predictable.

Everything clear? Great. Cycle of sin and military defeat. Breezy.

The last judge God sends, Samuel, is a busy guy. He pulls triple duty as a judge, prophet, and priest for God's people. As Samuel is getting up there in years, the Israelites decide they are ready for a leadership change.

> *Read 1 Samuel 8:1-5,19-20. What do the people cry out for? Why?*

## CHECK OUT THESE JUDGES OF ISRAEL

* Deborah (Judg. 4–5)
* Ehud (Judg. 3)
* Gideon (Judg. 6–8)
* Othniel (Judg. 3)
* Samson (Judg. 13–16)
* Shamgar (Judg. 3)

The people basically said, "Samuel, you're great and all, but your sons who you've given us as judges aren't good guys. They're not cutting it. We want a king. The other nations around us have them. We want a fancy king to lead us out into battle and fight for us." God warned them that it would be a mistake, but they wouldn't back down. *All the other nations have them ... Wahh ...*

So God gave them a king—Saul.

Saul waved from chariots and played the part of king like he was born for it. But in the end, it turns out he is a terrible king (and all around guy), so he finally gets ousted. Enter David.

David's the one who killed Goliath with a slingshot. Among other things. Impressive? Yes. But that's not actually what makes him so important.

* *Turn to 2 Samuel 7:1-17. Go ahead and read through it, and then we'll hit on the most important points.*

* *Let's look at verses 1-2. What does it seem David wanted to do for God?*

* *What does God promise David in verses 9-10?*

* *Now let's go over verses 12-16 together. Also, have I mentioned that this really will matter later even though it might seem like it's out of left field? What promises does God make to David?*

* *Who is God talking about in these verses?*

These verses tell us that a King will come from David's family, and He'll be King forever.

David preps to build God a ridiculously grand temple. But God tells him not to start the project.

* *Read 1 Chronicles 22:7-10. Why was David taken off the job?*

*Who was to take over?*

Ding, ding, ding. You're right. Solomon took over the project. It took about seven years to build the temple, and decades passed before it was completely finished. Some say it was the crowning achievement of Solomon's life and the pride of the Israelites.

When Solomon blessed the temple, he spoke words that pointed to the coming ages:

> But will God indeed dwell with man on the earth? Behold, heaven and the highest heaven cannot contain you, how much less this house that I have built!
> **2 CHRONICLES 6:18**

For years this was the temple where the Jewish people would go for worship, sacrifices, and feasts.

Before he died, David asked Solomon to:

> Be strong, and show yourself a man, and keep the charge of the LORD your God, walking in his ways and keeping his statutes, his commandments, his rules, and his testimonies ...
> **1 KINGS 2:2b-3a**

*Read 1 Kings 11:1-6. Did Solomon do what David asked? Explain.*

Unfortunately, Mr. Solomon loved the ladies a little too much. In fact, he had seven hundred wives, which I can only imagine made anniversary dinners complicated. He also had three hundred concubines. Why not? Most of these one thousand women came from foreign nations that the Lord had forbidden the Israelites to intermarry with.

Solomon's gals held a special place in their hearts for foreign gods. They convinced him to worship their gods too. And God called Solomon on it.

*Read 1 Kings 11:7-13. What did God tell Solomon He would do as a punishment for his sin?*

*What did God promise to Solomon in verse 13?*

MAP OF THE
DIVIDED
KINGDOM

OK, we're about to dive into a few straight paragraphs of historical facts. Hang in there with me. It's good stuff, promise.

Jacob's sons were each given a piece of land. (Remember our family tree on p. 20?) Each son had his own tribe; together they were known as the twelve tribes of Israel, and they made up the nation of Israel. But the nation of Israel split into two kingdoms—the Northern and the Southern Kingdoms. Ingenious naming, I know. From here on out, the Northern Kingdom goes by Israel and the Southern Kingdom by Judah.

You may notice that not every son is listed on this map. What happened to the land for Levi and Joseph? Great question. Levi didn't receive any land because he was part of the priesthood who considered the Lord their inheritance. And Joseph's land was given to his two sons, Manasseh and Ephraim. Got it?

In both kingdoms, it seemed like the throne room had a revolving door. Because of the leaders' and the people's disobedience, the two kingdoms both fell to foreign nations.

Not to get too into the details, but Judah (aka the Southern Kingdom) fell to the Babylonians who leveled Jerusalem and destroyed the temple.

Gone.

And not just the temple—they took the ark of the covenant as well, and it has never been recovered.

So now the Israelites are in exile, and to make a long story short, King Cyrus of Persia (who, conveniently enough had just overthrown the Babylonians) allowed a group of Israelites to go back and rebuild the temple. That Cyrus, what a guy!

When it was finished, there was a sadness that came along with the happiness of rebuilding—the temple was nowhere near as grand as Solomon's and the Israelites were devastated that it was such a shell of what had once been.

Before, during, and after the exile, God sent a message to the Israelites through people called prophets. The message was clear: *return to God.*

We'll leave it there for now, which probably seems strange since timeline-wise we're right here with the prophets. Don't worry, if you're really into prophets, we're actually going to talk more about them once we get to the New Testament. It'll make sense.

&ast; *Look at all of the names you've learned! Want to do a quick exercise before you close shop for the day? Find Matthew 1. We're going to highlight a couple names you might recognize.*

&ast; *Let's start with verse 2.*

*_____ was the father of _____, and _____ was the father of _____, and _____ was the father of _____.*

&ast; *And in verse 6:*

*_____ was the father of _____. And _____ was the father of _____.*

&ast; *Keep going and stop on verse 16.*

Yes. You guessed it. Our great King Jesus is in the lineage that we've been studying for the past few days, which will put us ahead of the game as we're talking through the New Testament.

The next time you open your book, you'll have traveled four hundred years.

We're going to take what we've learned and bring it with us into a new time and place. Once we get some background on what life looked like then (see, I promised you the hairstyles and fashions of the Old Testament would be important), we'll be ready to meet the Baby the world has been waiting for since one bite of fruit changed everything.

*two*

WEEK 2
# PREFACE: THE EARLY YEARS

The alternate title for this week was, "I'm sorry about your nativity set."

And here's where I tell you that some of what I learned for this study (not just for this week, but throughout) was actually shocking to me. I know, I know. Your confidence level is rising by the moment.

But that's honestly one thing that makes Scripture so fascinating:

You can never, ever, ever learn everything there is to know. There are always layers and symbolic references and correlations and metaphors and on and on. If you understand all of that and you're hungry for more, then have no fear: the entire Book of Revelation awaits you.

As you may have gathered, we're going to meet Jesus this week. Before we get started, I'm going to ask you to take a few minutes and think through what you understand about Mary's pregnancy and Jesus' birth—if this doesn't make for TV ratings, I don't know what does.

*Hey, Joseph. How was work? Did you like the lunch I packed? Did you talk to your boss about taking next Tuesday off so we can go donkey shopping? Also, I found out I'm going to deliver the Son of God.*

I joke, but the reality is that the details we rarely consider are actually what allow us to step into the story. Picture Mary and the baby Jesus. I'm going to go out on a limb and say you didn't picture Him screaming while Mary tells Joseph she has tried everything and He won't stop. She has run her fingers along His gums, and there aren't any teeth breaking through. *He's probably just overtired,* she thinks. *He does feel pretty warm, but He isn't listless. Should I take Him somewhere? Bathe Him?*

She is exhausted. It's the third night in a row that He's been inconsolable, and it's always when she lays Him down for bed. Finally it hits her: ear infection.

So she sits upright and rocks Him until He sighs and she feels His full weight press onto her. She doesn't move for hours, knowing it's the only way to keep Him asleep. As she pats His back over and over, she decides she'll go three houses down in the morning; Beth will make one of her concoctions, and it'll only be a few hours until He's back to His normal, happy self.

Motherhood isn't for the faint of heart.

Especially when you're raising the Messiah.

## GROUP SESSION GUIDE

### SESSION 2: REVIEW WEEK 1 HOMEWORK

\* What new truths did you learn from your homework this week?

\* Day 1: Think for a moment about Adam and Eve in the garden of Eden and the lie they believed. In what areas of your life right now do you wonder if God is really for you and if He has your best in mind?

\* Day 2: This day of study covered a lot of history for the people of God. How does seeing God's intentionality and presence in each of these circumstances make you feel? What might it say about His character, even in the hard seasons of life?

\* Day 3: Explain the story of the first Passover. Do you see threads of that story in other Bible passages? If you're just learning of the story, what about it stuck out to you?

\* Day 4: What's one of the best things that the law does for us? What about what it did for the people of Israel back in the day? How does that explain a bit of the culture that Jesus was born into?

\* Day 5: Did you learn anything new about Jesus' family tree and the history of Israel today? How does understanding Jesus' ancestry help you see Jesus in a new light?

**WATCH SESSION 2 (VIDEO RUN TIME 10:35)**

## DISCUSS

*What part of the video spoke to you the most? Why?

*Have you ever considered the way Jesus grew up? How He had to learn things like all children do? What do you think about that?

*Angie says, "Jesus spent more of His life as a student than a teacher." How does this truth speak into the places of your life where you're still learning and growing?

*Jesus allowed Himself to be humbled so that He could experience life the way His creation did. What does that tell us about Jesus' character and heart?

*This week, how will you live in the wonder of who Jesus is?

Video sessions available for purchase or rent
at *LifeWay.com/Matchless*

DAY 1

# THE CULTURAL CLIMATE

Welcome, welcome. I hope you had a great trip. Four hundred years have passed and things are going to look a little different around here. Let me give you a quick tour.

*Location of Israel*

world map

*Palestine*

Israel is also referred to as Palestine, a name the Greeks applied to the entire southeastern Mediterranean region.

There's a running joke in my family that I'll never be able to deny: maps scare me and my sense of direction is terrifyingly bad. Like, way worse than what you're picturing. I get lost on roads that are less than ten miles from my house. If I should take a wrong turn anywhere within those ten miles, I have no clue how to find my way. But I'm determined not to be afraid of these maps because, God bless them, they've been all alone in the back of the Bible for so long.

I confess, I'm reporting the following information based on the assessment of both my brilliant husband and my friend "The Google®."

So if you fall in the directionally-challenged camp, I'm with you. I'm for you.

Speaking of my husband, I must tell you the story of the day I decided that a one-thousand-piece puzzle would be a fun bonding experience for us as newlyweds. (I know, some of you are already shaking your heads.) I ended up realizing I had married a psychopath. You guys, he started with random pieces. WITH NO BORDERS. This kind of madness can only be dealt with by prayer and constant monitoring.

I mean, come on, everyone knows you have to get the shape and size of the puzzle before you start randomly piecing together people's heads and words (which, frankly, is also a cop-out from doing the hard work of sorting sixty-eight shades of blue sky) because they just won't make as much sense if they aren't in context.

The maps give us shape and size—context. So take a look at the maps; gaze at them. Now, make them your friends. (There's a giant map on the inside back cover of your Bible study book, too.)

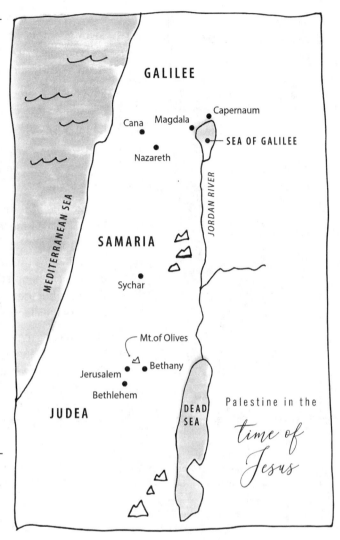

Palestine in the *time of Jesus*

Especially note the Palestine map because we'll be traveling around this area a lot. Mark this page because you'll be looking back when it's time to track our travels.

While we're looking around, let's remember that the temple was in Jerusalem.

*\* What do you remember about it from earlier in our study? This is a free-for-all, so just go for whatever comes to mind.*

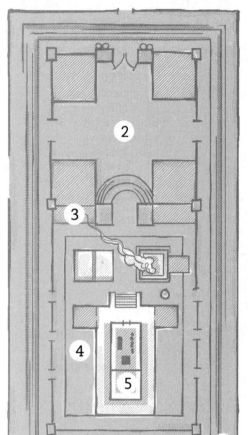

Now, let's take a closer look. And keep in mind this is the second temple. Not as spectacular as the original. There are a couple places I want you to notice: the court of the Gentiles, the court of women, and the holy of holies.

So you've memorized the layout of the temple and considered tattooing it on your person, yes? No. Well, that might not be the best choice.

And now for a wee bit of history. You're going to be really impressed with yourself at the end of today's work, so hang in there.

At the time of Jesus, the **Romans** were ruling over Israel. They allowed Israel to run its own little area, but only to a certain extent. The Jews were permitted to make decisions regarding their religious issues, but if it was a civil matter, the Romans handled it. The Romans weren't super fond of the Jews, but they needed to keep up a good relationship because their land was important for trade.

**Tiberius** was the emperor of Rome (which means he was the big guy) during the ministry of Christ. To make sure the Israelites weren't causing any trouble, the Romans sent down a representative to keep an eye on things and report back to Tiberius. The guy appointed for this fun job was **Pontius Pilate**, the governor of Judea.

*So let's make sure we've got this straight: Is Pontius Pilate a Roman or an Israelite?*

Perfect.

Rome also allowed a local guy there to rule over the people (he was considered their king), and his name was **Herod the Great**.

We're going to talk about him a little later, but for now, let's meet a few other people who are going to be on our radar for the next few months.

The first one is **Caiaphus**. He was the high priest. He's the top dog for the Jewish people, and he's basically considered the holiest guy around. What's funny is that the Jews didn't necessarily love the high priest because he was often in cahoots with the Romans.

*Was Caiaphus a Jew or a Roman?*

Let's keep trucking.

Underneath Caiaphus were a couple different groups of Jewish people. The first group was called the **Pharisees**. They were completely obsessed with making sure that everyone was obeying ALL of the laws, and they found great joy in correcting people who weren't. They were considered (especially by themselves) to be much holier than the "average" people because they were very well-educated about the Old Testament. They also liked to make up laws at their own leisure, which definitely made them a good hang.

Another religious group at the time was called the **Sadducees**. They were similar to the Pharisees, but unlike the Pharisees, they only accepted the written law (from the Torah) and not the oral tradition that had developed over time.

Another difference between the two is that most of the Sadducees didn't believe in resurrection or life after death. They didn't really want to deal with all the spiritual stuff—they preferred to live very opulent lives with a big focus on pleasure and wealth. I guess if you're only going to have this life, you want to whoop it up while you can.

*Write down your favorite food.*

Sorry—this stuff is dense and doesn't leave a whole lot of room for interaction. I really do care about you being involved.

OK, so these are the two big groups of religious sects. Now let's break it down some more:

The **scribes** were people who studied and interpreted the Law and taught others about it. They spent hours and hours copying the words of the Law with incredible precision (which is why we have such wonderful copies of the Old Testament). They could also draw up legal documents if needed. That fact will come in handy for them later in this story.

---

The main role of the **HIGH PRIEST** was to be in charge of the temple worship. Aaron was the first high priest, and his descendants were to continue to fill this role. Usually the high priest served for life. By Jesus' day, the office had lost its hereditary tie to Aaron. Herod the Great started appointing and dismissing the high priest as he saw fit. The Romans continued this practice, offering it to political favorites.

**ORAL TRADITION**

(also known as oral law or tradition of the elders), was a body of laws that were added to the written Law of Moses. They were only in oral form until written down in the Mishnah in the second century.[1] They were intended to help people know God's will in specific situations but instead ended up becoming burdensome and more overbearing than the law itself.[2]

Keep in mind that the general population at this time was illiterate, so they were dependent on those who could read in order to hear and understand Scripture.

And then there were the **zealots**. The zealots were men obsessed with the nation of Israel being independent, and they were SUPER into political stuff. As the name indicates, they were, umm, passionate.

And now to the **rabbis**. They were the religious heads of the synagogues, but they didn't really hold any power; they were more like educated spiritual and religious leaders.[3]

And now, the moment you have been waiting for … drumroll please.

The **Sanhedrin**. I know, I know. It's exciting(ish).

This one's going to be easy for you, though. The Sanhedrin is the highest Jewish council in the time of Jesus. It consists of seventy-one men (Sadducees and Pharisees) and the high priest was "the president" (you remember who that was, right?). These guys are called the elders.

Now listen. We're going to end with a quiz. If you want to cheat, just remember that God is watching you.

*What nation was ruling the Israelites?*

*What is the high priest's name?*

*Who is the emperor of Rome during Jesus' ministry?*

*What was Pontius Pilate sent to do in Judea?*

*Who was the local leader considered to be the Israelites' king?*

*What two groups made up the Sanhedrin?*

I've never been more proud of you. And I pinky promise this is the only day of study that has this much stuff that seems irrelevant. I'm well aware that you're going to either thank me or hate me later.

DAY 2
# BEFORE THE BIRTH

So here we are. One day away from meeting the Messiah.

I just want to reiterate this: you've done a lot of work to get here. My prayer is that because of that fact, you're going to see Jesus in a new way.

> *Before we get into the story, let's think back to the person who was considered the king of Judea. Do you remember his name? Clue: it ends with, "the Great."*

> *Read Luke 1:5 and high five yourself for reading it and understanding the context instead of skipping over it.*

> *Now read Luke 1:26-38 and try to put yourself in the story, imagining the details of the interaction.*

Most Christians can give a version of this story that hits the important details, but now we're going to commit to being curious about every word. That's my natural bent; I want to dig down deep because that's where the treasure is. So keep that in mind for this next activity.

> *Read that same section of Scripture again, and write down anything you didn't see the first time or something you're curious about.*

Good job. Unless it's empty. You're going to at least want to put a sentence in there in case other people think you are blowing off your homework.

I think we can probably agree this is a pretty jarring interaction for several reasons, not the least of which is that Mary's only about fifteen years old and is being told that she will be the mother of the Son of

God. After Gabriel tells her not to be afraid, he explains what is going to happen next.

Over and over, the angel uses definitive terms: "You have found favor with God ... you will conceive in your womb ... you shall call his name Jesus. He will be great and will be called the Son of the Most High ... God will give to him the throne of his father David, and he will reign over the house of Jacob forever, and of his kingdom there will be no end" (Luke 1:30-33).

Jacob, David—we know those names!

If you don't remember who they were, skip on back and read your notes. One of the prophets we'll be hanging out with today is Isaiah. And in case you forgot, prophets were chosen to warn the people and prophesy about what was to come even though they knew they would be rejected, hated, and possibly put to death.

*How was your day at work, Isaiah? For dinner we're going to have chicken and sadness.*

This icon indicates when a passage about Jesus' life points back to an Old Testament passage or prophecy.

**OT**

\* *Let's read what he wrote in Isaiah 7:14. Beautiful, isn't it?*

*Behold, the virgin shall conceive ...*

Immanuel, "God with us."

And just in case you wondered if Mary and Joseph took liberties with their Son's name, they didn't. Immanuel isn't a name—it's a description of the coming Child.

The Child we've been waiting for.

Mary doesn't question whether or not it's going to happen; she just wants to know how it will happen. I'll be honest, I'm not one hundred percent sure Gabriel's explanation would really make me feel confident about the whole thing.

Then Gabriel mentions that Mary's barren cousin, Elizabeth, is pregnant. It's a lot to take in, yes?

The only other words we hear her utter in the entire interaction are: "Behold I am the servant of the Lord; let it be to me according to your word" (Luke 1:38). She submits herself completely, bowing her heart to the will of God. Beautiful. Also dinner with Joseph is going to be awkward.

After Joseph learns of the pregnancy, he decides to divorce Mary quietly. (Did you catch that? Divorce his fiancée? How do you divorce someone you aren't married to? Turns out that in this time period, being engaged was a legal matter). Fortunately, an angel comes to him in a dream and clarifies that indeed, his fiancée will soon be carrying the Savior of the world. Aah. Got it. Makes sense now.

Interesting fact about Joseph? He never utters a single word in Scripture.

While we're on the subject of not speaking ...

Mary's cousin Elizabeth is married to a guy named Zechariah, and it turns out that Gabriel had also visited him to give him good news.

*Read Luke 1:11-23 and summarize what happens.*

**BETROTHAL**

Similar to an engagement to be married. However, in the first century, betrothal was as binding as marriage. It could only be broken through a divorce.[4]

On the surface it seems to be the exact same situation as Mary's, but in reality, Zechariah was expressing doubt, which is why God made him temporarily mute.

I can't help but notice random parts of the Bible that seem like they don't really have any real information. Like Luke 1:23. Basically he finished his day at work and went home. Why is that even recorded?

Well, if you think about it, the Gospels are being written and passed down based on eyewitnesses who were recording what they were seeing and experiencing. And here's something else I want you to keep in mind: these were ordinary people who were writing down a story based on true experiences.

They weren't writing "the Gospels." They were writing accounts of Jesus' story to tell people about what had happened. In no way did they imagine their work would eventually be combined and included in a book that would withstand thousands of years of scrutiny.

And now back to our story ... soon after Mary finds out she's pregnant, she travels to Judah, where her cousin Elizabeth is living, no doubt to see whether Elizabeth is pregnant. Keep in mind this trip isn't a walk across town. Elizabeth lived about eighty miles away. I'm not sure I would drive that far. And in the first months of pregnancy? That's going to be a no, Janet.

\* Read Luke 1:39-45. *What was the baby's reaction? What did Elizabeth proclaim?*

\* Now read Luke 1:67-75. *Who was Zechariah talking about here? How do you know?*

God had a special purpose for Elizabeth and Zechariah's baby boy. (We'll get to the rest of his story in a few days.) But isn't it interesting that this little family was the first to confirm what Gabriel had told Mary—the Child inside of her was the Messiah, the Savior of the world.

\* Read Luke 1:46-55. *How does Mary respond to Elizabeth's proclamation?*

Mary's praise in Luke 1:46-55 is often referred to as the Magnificat. This is Latin for the word *magnify*, which is the opening verb in her hymn.[5]

\* *Summarize what Mary says about God.*

\* *And how do her words point us back to the Old Testament?*

Mary offers a song of praise to God for what He had done and would do to fulfill what He had started hundreds of years before.

In a matter of days, this young woman and her humble carpenter husband would become a part of the greatest story of all time.

It will begin with what seems like an ordinary sentence:

> In those days a decree went out
> from Caesar Augustus that all the
> world should be registered.
> **LUKE 2:1**

## DAY 3
# THE BIRTH OF JESUS

And here we are. The place you probably thought the study was going to start. Today is the day we're going to meet our Messiah and learn more about His birth.

Here's the plan: as we go through the rest of Jesus' story, I'm going to ask you to look back in the Old Testament (a lot). You'll understand why I made you spend so much time back there. Don't worry, I'll have mercy and put some of the Scripture in your Bible study book.

\* *Quiz question (because we're going to be visiting them often): What was the job of the prophets?*

\* *One more: How much time has passed since the end of the Old Testament?*

We mainly started hearing from the prophets when the kingdom split, which was like eight hundred years before the time of Christ.

So they are way dead. And the people after them are way dead.

Great.

Here we are in Nazareth, where Mary and Joseph live. While Mary was pregnant, there was a census taken—the Census of Quirinius if you're curious—that ordered everyone to return to their hometowns in order to be "recorded." These head counts could take years because of the huge number of people and logistics of travel.

\* *Read Luke 2:1-5. Where were Mary and Joseph living at the time of the census?*

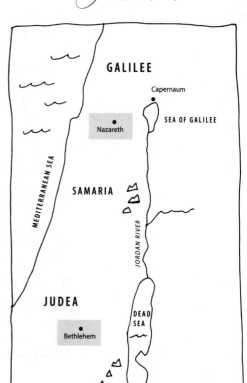

*Nazareth & Bethlehem*

*Where did they have to travel?*

**BETHLEHEM**

Means "house of bread"

Joseph's family line is traced back to King David (remember him?), whose ancestral home was Bethlehem. So even though Joseph and Mary are living in Nazareth, they have to travel back to Bethlehem to register. When they arrive, there's no room for them "in the inn" (likely because of the census), so Mary gives birth to Jesus in an unexpected location. We don't have a single detail of the actual birth, only the fact that after He was born He is swaddled up and placed in what may have been an animal's feeding trough.

You have a visual of all of this, no doubt. I'm going to apologize before I go any further because if you spent good money on your nativity set, you're going to be disappointed, and also you're likely not going to get a refund.

*Read Luke 2:7. Where does it say He was born in a manger? Whoops. It doesn't. It says He was laid in a manger, not that He was necessarily born in one.*

Some believe that it's more likely He was born in a cave.[6] Really—a cave.

*Let's rewind for a second. Do you remember when the Jewish people were going through the cycles of sin? What kind of Savior do you think they were expecting?*

I'll award you one point for "not an infant" and two for "a military leader." The Jewish people had been waiting for their coming King. And by "King" they meant a political powerhouse who would swoop in and rescue them from oppression. Someone wielding a sword and an agenda. Someone who would show up like a lightning bolt and defend them from their enemies.

Not a Baby being born next to livestock.

He could have done anything He wanted, but He came to earth as a wriggly, screaming, hungry, defenseless infant. He blinked, no doubt, as His newborn eyes tried to adjust to the light of the world around Him. And His mother held Him as she would any other child.

Within a few hours of His entrance into the world, the first birth announcement went out.

* Read Luke 2:8-20. What was the wording of the announcement, and who received it?

The glory of the Lord shone around a field of never-named shepherds while they watched their flock during the night. (Basically they kept an eye on the sheep so that none escaped or got attacked by another animal.)

The first shepherd in the Bible was Adam and Eve's son Abel (Gen. 4:2).

* Here's an interesting fact about shepherds. Look up Genesis 46:34. What does it say?

In the version of the Bible I'm reading right now, it sounds a bit confusing. In case yours is that way too, let me break it down: shepherds were considered unclean.[7] They're touching animals and dead things, and they don't wash properly. They are essentially outcasts who aren't allowed to associate with regular people. In general, the reputation of your average shepherd was not stellar.

The Bible talks about shepherds or shepherding more than two hundred times.[8]

So maybe don't toss the shepherds from your manger scene, but it would be a nice touch to scuff them up a little next Christmas and keep them away from the other people.

After the angel tells them not to be afraid (which is a pattern in Scripture for somewhat obvious reasons), he speaks words that have always existed but had never been uttered:

Fear not, for behold, I bring you good news of great joy that will be for all the people. For unto you is born this day in the city of David a Savior, who is Christ the Lord. And this will be a sign for you: you will find a baby wrapped in swaddling cloths and lying in a manger.
**LUKE 2:10b-12**

Who on earth is David, and why is he even in this story? We know nothing of this man.

*Or do we ...*

    ✳ *What do you remember about our friend King David?*

Right. So why does the angel say "city of David?" Welp, turns out he was born in Bethlehem, where Christ had just been born.

I'm guessing that the Jews were also not expecting the first announcement of His birth to be to a bunch of nasty shepherds.

But here's the part we want to take with us as we go; there is nothing in Scripture that doesn't mean something. The shepherds don't really seem that interesting, but they do seem unlikely.

Except ...

Some scholars believe those shepherds were keeping watch over a very specific type of sheep, one considered more precious than others.

These lambs were to be used for sacrifice in the temple, and in order for them to be an appropriate offering, they had to be perfect—without blemish.[9]

You'll never guess how they were protected after they were born: They were wrapped in swaddling cloths.

The spotless Lamb who will be sacrificed on our behalf, inviting the shepherds to be the first to see Him.

It seems like a strange way to do it, doesn't it?

And herein lies the beauty of the life and love of Christ.

Everyone assumed that Jesus would reveal Himself to those whom the world knew and recognized.

What the world never expected was that He would instead reveal Himself as King to lowly, obscure shepherds.

What He knew, of course, was that they were the ones who would recognize Him.

DAY 4
# AFTER JESUS' BIRTH

When last we chatted, the shepherds were meeting the Messiah in Bethlehem after an angel told them that their Savior had come. I might as well go ahead and tell you He wasn't born on December 25, nor was it likely He was born in winter.

Remember from our study yesterday that after the shepherds saw the baby Jesus, they started telling anyone who would listen that Jesus had been born (Luke 2:17-18). Here's what's interesting: shepherds (as a whole) "were considered unreliable and were not allowed to give testimony in the law courts."[10]

So let's summarize: the first people who saw the Lord were lower-class, unclean, insignificant, unreliable, and powerless people.

In other words, the people He came to save.

\* *Before we move on, let's write down where Jesus was born.*

Now keep in mind that Mary and Joseph weren't from that town. They had only gone there because of the census decree.

\* *Find Micah 5 and read verses 2-5a. How does this passage*  *speak to the coming of Jesus?*

Hmm. The Savior will be born in Bethlehem, will be a ruler in Israel, his brothers will return to the people of Israel, he will shepherd them ... sounds like Jesus, doesn't it?

We know very little about the days after Christ's birth, but we do know a few important facts.

\* *Read Luke 2:21. What happened on the eighth day of His life?*

That feels like a lot of information. Not exactly the kind of thing I would make sure to include in the very limited amount of detail we're offered about Him, but I didn't write it. So why is this so important?

✴ *Hop on over to Leviticus 12:2-3. What's commanded?*

Jesus was circumcised in accordance with Jewish law. It showed His connection to God's people and was a sign of His humanity. He was "born under the law, to redeem those who were under the law" (Gal. 4:4-5).

✴ *Continue reading in Leviticus 12 until you finish verse 8.*

There was a lot going on for these ladies for a few weeks, huh?

Alright, let's skip past those pleasantries and write down some details.

PURIFICATION PERIOD

"A woman who bore a son was ceremonially unclean for 40 days (twice that if she bore a daughter)."[11]

✴ *When her purification period was over, what was she to do? (See Lev. 12:6.)*

*She shall bring to the* _____ *and offer a*

_____ *for a burnt offering, and a*

_____ *or* _____ *for a sin offering.*

✴ *Although this was the law, there is a stipulation for those who are too poor to offer an unblemished lamb. Read Leviticus 12:8 again, paying close attention to what it says. What's the stipulation?*

✴ *Now let's skip back over to Luke 2 and read verses 23-24. What does this tell us about Mary and Joseph?*

So now we're really off-track from what the Jews were expecting in a Messiah. Let's add "poor" to the ever-growing list of reasons this couldn't be their guy.

* You remember the temple, right? Who wanted to build the first temple?

* Who actually built it?

* What happened to that first temple?

* When the Jews were in exile, what were they permitted to do?

* How did it compare to the original?

Good.

So even though it's hundreds of years later, this is the same temple we learned about earlier. When Herod the Great (who was an infamously well-known and respected builder) came to power, he decided he would go one step further in his "Let's just get along" plan. He began MASSIVE renovations of the temple that took several years to finish. This temple was the temple of Jesus' day.

While Joseph and Mary are in the temple, they meet a few special people who God had appointed to be a part of Jesus' life.

The first is Simeon, who was told by God that he wouldn't die before he had laid eyes on the Messiah. We aren't told how old he was, only that he came to the temple under the direction of the Holy Spirit, took the Baby into his arms, and praised God.

* Read Luke 2:29-35. In verse 32, what does it say Jesus will be?

OK, next one up to bat is a sweet lady by the name of Anna, who, God bless, (literally) had been living in the temple for years. Although that's the language used, it's very likely that she didn't actually live there but had made it her highest priority to spend her time there. We know that she's old and that she's a widow, and we know that she spent all of her days and nights worshiping, fasting, and praying for the Savior of the world. Well, lo and behold, she finally sees Him and recognizes Him immediately. She gives thanks to God and tells everyone who has been waiting for the One who will bring their redemption that He's come.

Who have we forgotten to mention? Ah—the three wise men who came to see Jesus. All I know is that frankincense was involved, and I would only endure the smell because sweet baby Jesus was there.

> *What did they bring? (I helped you out a bit.)
>
> _____, _____,
>
> and _____ (Matt. 2:11).

Actually, sweet Baby Jesus wasn't much of a Baby by the time the wise men brought their gifts. He was a toddler by then probably, and we can only hope that He has avoided frankincense for the last few years.

I know, I know. It's crazy but true. As a matter of fact, one of my dear friends (who is a pastor) puts the wise men on the other side of the room from the manger.

And while we're talking about our crumbling nativity sets, there weren't just three wise men.

I know there are three wise men in that gorgeous display you have, but alas, there were probably more of them. Maybe even WAY more. I think the three gifts thing throws us off. We assume three gifts, three people. But nowhere in Scripture mentions there were only three magi.

It's just that there isn't room in the shaped Styrofoam® packaging to fit all of these folks.

Incidentally, both of our nativity goats lost two legs this year, and a new figurine featuring a man with a bagpipe showed up in the box—and none of us know where he came from. But we felt bad for him so we just set him in the back. I don't think we've gone a single year without a missing limb or accessory.

If you're keeping track, the baby shower has now included a young virgin mother and her husband, some dirty shepherds, and a random man and woman who had been praying for the coming of the Messiah. There may or may not have been bagpipes.

I'm going to go out on a limb and say none of them brought monogrammed onesies or cakes made of diapers.

What must Mary and Joseph have been thinking? Just a dirt poor couple trying to follow the law. So poor that they couldn't afford to bring a spotless lamb to the temple to be killed as a sacrifice.

It would be years before they knew the truth—that they had, in fact, done exactly that.

DAY 5
# JESUS' CHILDHOOD

After Jesus has been presented at the temple in Jerusalem,
a little bit of a wild goose chase ensues.

> *Read Matthew 2:1-12. Why did the wise men show up in
> Jerusalem?*

> *Summarize Herod's reactions to the news that a new King
> had been born.*

Ah, Herod the Great. (Remember him? You're basically his best friend
right now. Which isn't exactly amazing because someone once said it
was better to be his pig than his son.)

As you may recall, the man likes power. The Savior of the world coming
would certainly put a kink in his plans for world domination.

> *Do you remember what Pharaoh did back in Exodus when
> he thought the Israelites were multiplying too quickly?*

Herod has a similar plan. He tells the wise men to track the Baby down
and report back, but they don't obey him. He is NOT PLEASED about this
development and orders all the boys in Bethlehem under the age of two
to be killed.

> *Read Matthew 2:16-18. Which prophecy did this event fulfill?*

*Read Matthew 2:13-15,19-23. How do you see God protecting Jesus and unfolding the plan of redemption?*

All right, so fortunately, God likes to talk to Joseph while he's sleeping. He warns Joseph to get out of Bethlehem and go to Egypt. They stay in Egypt until after Herod the Great dies. Then God uses another dream to give Joseph the next step.

*Where was Joseph supposed to take his family (v. 20)?*

*How did this move from Egypt back to Israel also fulfill prophecy (v. 15)?*

Sounds reasonable, right? Let's pack it up and head back to Israel.

*So Joseph obeys, and then God gives him further instructions (you'll never guess how) in a dream, warning Joseph not to go to Judea. Why not (v. 22)?*

## ARCHELAUS

When Herod the Great died, his kingdom was split among his sons. Archelaus was the oldest and ruled in Judea. He was known for his cruelty, so Mary and Joseph moved on to live in Galilee.[12]

Herod just won't leave us alone, will he? Now it's his son Archelaus who's the problem.

*Where did Joseph then take his family? It's a district of Galilee ...*

*What was fulfilled by this happening (v. 23)?*

I mean, you have to admit that the odds of all of this just happening coincidentally are pretty insurmountable. And don't worry, it's going to get even better.

We don't know much about the childhood of Jesus outside of a few events.

*Here's what we do know: hop on over to Luke 2:39-40.
What does it say?*

*Jesus _____ and became _____, filled with _____. And the _____ of _____ was upon Him.*

Here come the biggest questions of all: When did Jesus know that He was the Son of God? Was He the perfect Child? Did He ever talk back or get in trouble?

I will not pretend to be an expert on any of this—quite frankly because there are too many gaps to make any conclusive statements about His childhood.

So what was He like? Here is what we do know:

According to Luke 2:52, Jesus was a well-rounded kid. He grew mentally (wisdom), physically (stature), spiritually (favor with God), and socially (favor with people.)

Jesus was born sinless, and Scripture says that although He was tempted, He did not sin. Now, was He capable of sin? That deep theological question has been around for centuries, with solid scholarship on both sides of the issue. I believe Jesus couldn't sin because of the nature of God. He could be tempted, but it would be against His character to sin.

So what's sin with regard to an infant or child? My remedial definition would be anything that's willful disobedience.

For example, Jesus may have accidentally run into another child while they were playing or broken a dish, but He never actually sinned.

It's a hard concept, isn't it? I mean, if He was God, then He was born with all of the knowledge of God. True. But He was also fully man. In my head, I imagine it to be a situation where God chose to limit the knowledge His Son had in order to allow Him to experience life the way that any other little boy would have.

If so, Jesus probably didn't know that He was the Son of God for a good bit of His early years. When Scripture says He "grew" in the previous verse, and later that he "increased in wisdom and in stature" (Luke 2:40,52), I believe it's an indication that He continued to learn how to be strong and wise—all the while with the favor of God resting on Him.

But, at the age of twelve, we see a shift in His development that marks the first time we hear Him hint at His deity.

*Let's start with reading Luke 2:41-48. You will surely be blessed. Write down a summary of what you read.*

YOU GUYS, THEY LOST THE MESSIAH.

Let's just break this down for a hot second. Not only did they lose Him, it wasn't an "I swear he was just in the shoe section, and now I'm panicked for three minutes in Target®" kind of thing.

As a sidebar: I definitely lost one of my identical twin daughters in a bookstore once, and in my desperation I ran from aisle to aisle with the other one on my hip. I looked up and saw Tim McGraw (because Nashville), and he just started looking around until we both saw her. It was fairly obvious that she belonged to me, given that I was holding her clone.

I also lost Kate at Disney World® once too. I found her in the "lost and found" coloring a picture of Goofy with all the other kids who had slacker parents.

Next up for me is a parenting book. Stay tuned.

But listen, each of those incidents (while they felt like an eternity) lasted no more than a few minutes.

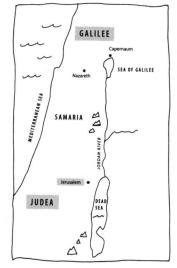

They didn't realize for an entire day that Jesus wasn't with them. Where's Brad Paisley when you need him?

In Mary and Joseph's defense, there was a huge group of family members traveling together, and I guess she just thought Jesus was somewhere in the herd. But when they stopped for the night, they realized He wasn't with them.

Am I the only one who imagines Mary looking up all *Home Alone* style and shouting, "JESUS!"?

Anyway, they retrace their steps back to Jerusalem (which took another day, so they must have been out of their minds with worry). When they finally find him in the temple, they see Jesus finishing up a masterpiece of Minnie Mouse® while all of the other kids are annoyed because He stayed in the lines. You know He stayed in the lines.

Actually, no. They find Him in the temple having intellectual conversations with the rabbis, while people around Him were amazed at His knowledge. And in this moment He began to reveal that He wasn't, in fact, a typical twelve-year-old. Even His parents were astonished, which seems to infer that this was the first time they had seen Him in this light.

*Of course, you must read the rest of verse 48 again and then keep going until you finish through verse 52. Did Mary react like a normal parent? Explain.*

*What did Jesus mean by His response?*

Mary reprimanded Jesus in a way not so dissimilar to the way we might react to our children. But Jesus responded with what I'm sure to Mary seemed like cryptic words that essentially put the wheels of His ministry in motion.

*What were those words?*

The first words we hear from Jesus—and they're in the form of a question:

Why were you looking for me? Did you not know that I must be in my Father's house?
LUKE 2:49

I know that Jesus is a young boy here. But I realized that for some reason when I imagine this story—when Jesus tells Mary and Joseph that they should have known He would be in His Father's house—I've always pictured Him as a man and not a twelve-year-old.

It feels different to imagine a boy looking into His parents' eyes and telling them in so many words that this was the beginning of what they always knew would come.

Because to them Jesus was the baby who took His first steps while they clapped.

*He was the toddler who ran around barefoot in the grass and learned to put His head underwater.*

*He was the three-year-old who laughed until His stomach hurt and loved being thrown in the air.*

*He was the five-year-old who begged for bedtime stories and forehead kisses.*

*He was the seven-year-old who ran to His father when he came home from work and woke up before the sun.*

*He was the nine-year-old who was brave enough to walk to a friend's house but looked back at His mother the whole way as she smiled and waved Him on.*

*He was the ten-year-old who decided He was too old for bedtime stories and public hugs and never knew that His mother cried because it meant He wasn't a baby anymore.*

It's how it is for all of us; we can't keep them small.

But imagine Mary—beautiful, young, devout Mary, her eyes shining and heart pounding as her Son reminded her He is someone else's Son.

Yes, He is the Great I am. But what mother can forget who He was?

Son of Mary, sent to be born.

Son of Man, sent to take on flesh.

Son of Sorrow, sent to die.

Son of God, sent to be risen to save us all.

Mary, your hands have been loosed; you have raised Him.

three

WEEK 3

# PRESENCE: STARTING HIS MINISTRY

We're going to cover a lot this week. Now that we know a little bit about who Jesus was as a child, we're going to see who He grew up to be.

You're going to get sick of hearing me say this—I don't need your feedback, Janet—but our goal in this study is not to memorize a bunch of facts and walk away or memorize a couple of verses and get the gist of the general time line of Christ's life. We want to meet Him where He is on every page and make sure that we are paying attention to the small things. We need to remind ourselves that every single word is purposeful and intended to show us both His humanity and His divinity. He wasn't a far-off God who barked orders; He was a confidante, friend, teacher, and compassionate man who people knew they could always come to when they were confused or walking through grief.

He spent three years of His life with the same group of people. (Are you sure you really know who they are? I'm going to warn you. If you have a seasonal display of Jesus walking through the desert with His pals, you might have some rearranging to do this week.)

Before we even meet those guys, we're going to see Jesus being tested by Satan for forty days. Remember, when you see the number forty in Scripture, it indicates testing. True story.[1] After Jesus came out of the wilderness, He was going to meet up with His cousin and officially kick-start His ministry.

Again, let's pull back the lens.

Jesus walked alongside men He had invited to partner with Him, all the while knowing what His future held.

He also knew that no matter how much they declared they would never abandon Him, every single one would. He knew which one would betray Him and which one would deny Him.

And He loved them in spite of it.

There was no way for them to lose His love, despite the fact that they didn't deserve it.

Turns out that's His specialty.

# GROUP SESSION GUIDE

## SESSION 3: REVIEW WEEK 2 HOMEWORK

\* What new things did you grasp from the Scripture this week in your homework?

\* Day 1: Just for fun, pick your favorite religious group that we discussed this week—Pharisees, Sadducees, scribes. Explain why you like them.

\* Day 2: Put yourself in Mary's shoes for a minute. How do you think you'd have reacted to the angel Gabriel's decree?

\* Jesus is Immanuel, God with us. Tell your group about a hard situation you're in right now. How do you think Jesus' presence with you changes your experience?

\* Day 3: Did you throw away part of your nativity set after this day of study? But really, did you?

\* So much of Jesus' story seems unlikely to our ears—the manger situation and the shepherds—and we're just getting started. Think about a time in your life when you saw God work in an unlikely way. Tell your group about it; how did He come through for you?

\* Day 4: Describe the story of Anna and Simeon, the folks we meet in the temple. What did their devotion to God look like? How did Jesus play a part (other than being God)?

*Day 5: Jesus was God, sinless, but He was also fully man. If you want your head to explode, try to figure out how all of that works. Then tell me. How does Jesus' humanity help you feel His empathy and understanding for your frailty and need? Does it bring you comfort? Freak you out? (All answers are welcome here.)

**WATCH SESSION 3 (VIDEO RUN TIME 10:31)**

## DISCUSS

*What part of the video resonated with you the most? Why?

*Jesus' compassion moved Him to action in the lives of those around Him. Do you "see" the people around you with compassion? Especially those who may not "have it all together"?

*Think about the woman with the issue of blood whom Jesus healed. Do you ever hesitate to bring your needs to Jesus? Why?

*Angie says, "Sometimes we want to be healed, but we don't necessarily want to tell people what we've been healed of." Are you sometimes reluctant to share what Jesus has healed you of? Explain.

*How are you encouraged to live differently because Jesus sees you with compassion?

Video sessions available for purchase or rent
at *LifeWay.com/Matchless*

DAY 1
# BAPTISM

John was called **"the Baptist"** because he baptized people, not because he was
a charter member of First Baptist Church of Jerusalem.

John, the cousin of Jesus, had the best dating app profile in the history of the world:

"Hi, I'm John. You might know my cousin, Jesus. I'm a wilderness guy, and I love the water. I'm looking for someone who likes a guy dressed in camel hair and leather belts. My dad was a priest named Zechariah, which was supposed to be my name, but then my dad went mute for awhile. He got his voice back, though. You might have heard me yelling, 'Repent!' while you were in town. We can talk more about that over a nice plate of locusts."

Seriously—this guy. Talk about the least likely person to begin the official ministry of the Son of God.

Let's start at the beginning and get to know him a little bit. Although he is recognized by the name "John the Baptist," there's a lot more to him and the role he plays in the life of Jesus.

As a quick side note, the John we are discussing today is *not* the same John who wrote the Gospel of John. However, Gospel-John did write about Baptist-John. Got it? Perfect. If not, don't worry, you will.

Flip over to the beginning of the Book of Luke. Luke is a physician, and he's very factual and cuts to the chase if you will.

   * *Read Luke 1:1-4. Write a brief summary of everything it says.*

I'm kidding. If you tried, I'll give you extra credit and my Netflix® password.

   * *Here's the bottom line (you can get this one): Who does Luke mention in verse 3?*

You may be surprised to know that the Gospel of Luke is actually a letter that Luke wrote to his friend, Theophilus.

   * *Now turn to Acts 1:1. Who is it addressed to?*

The Book of Acts is also written by Luke as a letter to Theophilus. There are a lot of theories about who Theophilus was, ranging from a high-powered lawyer to a Roman official to Luke's supporter who paid to have the book published, or maybe even a priest.[2] The truth is that there were several people in this time period who were named Theophilus. The fact that Luke addresses him as "most excellent," might indicate he was a man of high rank, but really it's impossible to know who Luke was specifically referring to.[3]

So other than knowing that he's Luke's pen pal, there isn't much to learn.

*Now read Luke 1:5 and fill in the blanks below.*

*In the days of _____, king of _____, there was a priest named Zechariah ...*

I'm going to guess that you've skimmed over that verse as something that isn't really necessary to know—and also it's confusing and who are all of these people?

If you've been doing your homework up until now, give yourself a round of applause.

We know Herod the Great, right? OK, that's who Luke is talking about here.

We know he was king of Judea.[4] We know that Zechariah was a priest and also the father of John the Baptist. And according to Luke 1:39, they lived in "a town in the hill country of Judah" (CSB).

These events are taking place in a specific time, in a specific place. It isn't just a little fairy tale; it's world history.

For the sake of time, I'm going to do a quick summary of John's life.

Zechariah is working in the temple when the angel Gabriel appears to him. (Remember Gabriel? Yes, he's the same angel who will tell Mary she's going to bear God's Son.) Gabriel lets Zechariah know that his wife is going to have a baby, and he must name the baby John. This is pretty surprising news to Zechariah because Elizabeth is barren, and they are both "well along in years" (Luke 1:18, CSB).

*Read Luke 1:18-20. How does Zechariah respond to Gabriel?*

## PRIESTLY DUTIES

There were twenty-four divisions of priests. Each division served twice a year for a week at a time, and then all the priests served during the major festivals of Passover, Pentecost, and Feast of Tabernacles.

\* *What is the cost of this response?*

\* *Read Luke 1:34. How does Mary respond to Gabriel's news to her?*

\* *Is there a difference between Zechariah's response and Mary's response? Explain.*

His response doesn't sound that different from Mary's on paper, but Zechariah's is a question of doubt. He expresses disbelief, whereas Mary's question is one born out of confusion. Gabriel punishes him for his disbelief. Zechariah immediately becomes mute and stays that way until the day the baby is circumcised and his name is announced.

When it comes time to name the baby, everyone assumes his name would be Zechariah because in that day the firstborn sons were typically named after the father. But Elizabeth quickly tells them that his name is John (Luke 1:60). They are confused, and they look to Zechariah to signal whether or not that's true. So he motioned for a writing tablet and scratched the words, "His name is John."

Immediately, his tongue was loosened, and he began to prophesy, telling them that his son would have an indelible mark on all of time, as would the One who would come after John. We looked at some of these verses earlier, but let's take a look at them again.

\* *Read his words in verses 67-79. Which verses speak of Jesus and what does Zechariah prophesy about Him?*

\* *Which verses speak of John? What would be his role?*

An otherwise obscure priest has just written his son's name on a tablet and declared that this baby will make way for the Lord. He will go before Him. He will prepare the people to hear the message Christ has. Not your typical scenario.

Do you remember when we briefly mentioned the prophets from the Old Testament? Remember: the prophets lived hundreds of years before Christ came, and part of their job was to warn the people that the Savior was coming and they must repent of their sin.

*Go to Isaiah 40:3-5. Write it below.

*Now go back to Luke 3:1-6 and note the fulfillment of that Isaiah passage.

I don't know why certain phrases move me as I'm reading Scripture, but Isaiah 40:6a does.

A voice says, "Cry!"

And I said, "What shall I cry?"

I suppose I relate to John's eager, earnest, and yet unsure response.

I imagine God said to him:

*Cry out to them, John. Cry out to the people who have forgotten God and given up on being rescued. Cry out from the depths of your heart and tell them that the true King of the Jews is coming for His people.*

*Tell them I know some have forgotten about Me for hundreds of years, and it has grieved Me. Explain that you aren't Me and that what I will bring is better than water; it is my Holy Spirit and the promise of salvation.*

*Tell them that they have to repent, and, as a sign of that repentance, they will be dipped under water and brought back up. Tell them that their Christ will be baptized in the same water, that they are living in the very days of the Messiah's appearance.*

*Prepare the Way of the Lord.*

> ✳ Read Mark 1:4-8 and Luke 3:7-18. Summarize the message John the Baptist was preaching to the people.

John preached a message of repentance. He pointed to the One coming after him who would change everything.

And one day, in the midst of hundreds of people, John looked up into the eyes of that One. God in flesh, standing before him. He says, *Here is the Lamb of God, who takes away the sin of the world!* (John 1:29). When Jesus asks John to baptize Him, John hesitates but obeys Jesus. When Jesus comes out of the water, immediately the sky opens up, and the voice of God speaks:

> You are my beloved Son;
> with you I am well pleased.
> **MARK 1:11**

Don't rush through this story without putting yourself in it. Don't just tuck it away as another fact you have on hand in case it comes up in Bible study.

Picture the crowds staring as John wraps an arm around his cousin— the One whom the world has waited for. The One whom John has been carving a path to ready the world for.

For one split second, the weight of Jesus is being lowered and lifted by a mere man.

What they saw was another soaking-wet man coming up from the water. But soon they would learn that He truly is the beloved Son, and He came to lower Himself to lift us.

How can it be?

DAY 2
# TEMPTATION

"Hardly had the voice from heaven died away then we hear a whisper from hell."[5]

I would venture to say that we have all felt this to a certain extent.

The fact of the matter is that there is a real, true battle going on in the spiritual realm, and we are constantly caught in the middle of it.

I don't know where you are in your walk with Jesus, but maybe, if you're just putting your toe in the water with this study, you just decided the whole thing sounds a bit creepy. Really? A cosmic battle? That sounds like a great movie plot but pretty far removed from real life.

Truly, though, it's an accurate commentary on the way our enemy gets to us. Make it sound ridiculous. Dismiss him. See him as a character portrayed on Halloween with red-faced masks and horns. Then file him in the same category as all of the other villains wandering around the neighborhood on October 31.

Dull him down.

Or better yet, pretend he doesn't exist. Act like he's just a costume.

I guess I came to faith in a way that made me very suspicious of this kind of thing. Who is naive enough to believe in the devil or delusional enough to create his existence?

Might I confess that I saw the whole thing as fantastical and chalked it up to another weird thing Christians believed?

Might I also confess that on occasion I still wonder if the whole thing is true?

Now before you decide I'm a heretic, hear me out. (Don't bother writing me hate mail. I have an amazing assistant and I will never see it.) Can you tell me that in the entire history of your being a Christian, you have never once had a moment of questioning related to your faith?

If you answered yes to my question—congratulations! You're a liar.

Too harsh? Listen, Janet, maybe you trusted Jesus for your salvation one day and have never looked back. Or doubted. Or questioned. If that's your story, I'm genuinely so glad for you.

**Four** in **ten** Millennials agree strongly or somewhat with the statement, "The devil, or Satan, is not a real being but is just a symbol of evil."[6]

That's not the case for a lot of us.

God knows we won't have unswerving, perfected, never-doubting faith. If that's a box you've felt trapped in, let this be your moment of release. God knows you aren't perfect; He doesn't keep you at arm's length in the moments you feel like you're failing. In fact, He chose to submit Himself to the same temptations we do so that He could fully experience His humanity and relate to ours.

Again—does this faith stuff sound more like a sci-fi movie than a historical statement? If so, you aren't alone in feeling that way.

*Jump to Matthew and read 4:1-11. Where was Jesus led?*

*By whom?*

*Who was He being tested by?*

Does this story sound cruel to you? The Holy Spirit called Him into the wilderness to be tested by Satan? Really? Why?

Don't worry; I have all of the answers, and I am willing to share my insights with you because you forked out cash for this study, and I don't want you to leave empty-handed.

That's not exactly accurate, but I would love nothing more than for you to finish this study with the belief that you can read and understand Scripture without fancy commentaries or brilliant pastors. These are both amazing resources that we can learn from, but they are not necessary in order for you to read the Word and take it in.

*How long did Jesus fast?*

*What did He feel by the end?*

But wait, He's God. He doesn't need food because He already has everything. He isn't dependent on food to fill Him; He is full.

And yet He humbled Himself to experience what we do. He wanted to feel our feelings, our longings, our sadness, our struggles …

Though divine, He chose to live in our flesh.

* *Let's look closely at the text: When does it say that Satan showed up to test Jesus? Was it right when He got to the desert?*

Not according to the story we read in Scripture. It seems that the devil waited until Jesus was desperate for food, and then he was more than happy to offer it to Jesus.

There's no point in trying to tempt someone with food if that person has just finished Thanksgiving dinner. It's easy to avoid desire if you're in a position of little need.

No one who is in an ecstatically healthy marriage has an affair. No one who has her dream job decides to quit for no reason. Satan isn't going to bank on those folks; he's going to wait until trouble is brewing. Until a wife feels unappreciated by her husband and a co-worker shows her the affection she's been craving.

He's too smart to show up on day one. He waits until we are desperate, lonely, doubting, and depressed.

He waits until we have reason to believe that God has chosen not to rescue us from our situation.

He waits until we have more weakness than faith. Then he bursts wide open the door that we don't always realize we've left cracked for him.

* *What are the first seven words we hear Satan say to Jesus?*

Now listen. Satan knows very well that this is Jesus.

Here Satan is tempting Jesus to misuse His authority as the Son of God.[7] He's not asking Jesus to prove that He is Christ; Satan's trying to appeal to Jesus' humanity the same way he appealed to Adam and Eve.

* *What is the first thing Satan tried to get Jesus to do?*
  *Verse 3:*
  *"If you are the Son of God ... "*

* *Why do you think Satan used this to test Him?*

* *How does Jesus respond?*

* *Use the same format with the other temptations.*

* *Second temptation:*
  *Verse 6:*
  *"If you are the Son of God ... "*

* *Satan's purpose:*

* *Jesus' response:*

* *Third temptation:*
  *Verse 9:*
  *"If you will fall down and worship me ... "*

*Satan's purpose:*

*Jesus' response:*

With the first temptation, Satan tried to get Jesus to provide for Himself instead of relying on God. In the second temptation, Satan tried to get Jesus to test God's faithfulness by forcing God to act. And with the third temptation, the enemy offered Christ a "better plan."

Satan tried to take advantage of Christ's humanity, and Christ refused to succumb.

*How do you see the enemy using the same kinds of tactics in tempting you?*

> [Satan] departed from him until an opportune time.
> **LUKE 4:13b**

So the angel who had fallen from heaven retreated once again. Then the long-awaited Savior began to walk—to the disciples, the crowds, the miracles, the love, the desperation, the agony, and the purposes for which He came.

With every step, He was closer to the story that has trickled all the way to this very moment in our lives, to the Man who loves us more than we understand and paid the highest price for those who believe Him.

But I won't get too far ahead of myself; let's listen to the story for ourselves.

> For because he himself has suffered when tempted, he is able to help those who are being tempted.
> **HEBREWS 2:18**

DAY 3
# GOSPELS

I'm coming in like a wrecking ball on this one. Deep breath.
I have a feeling you might be a little rattled by today's content.
And here we go.

There are four different people who wrote about the life of Jesus. Their writings are the first four books of the New Testament and are called the Gospels. I'm not sure how you imagine that; for a long time I just sort of saw them as facts on paper and didn't necessarily think about them as documents written for specific purposes. These writers had no idea that their accounts of Jesus' life would end up in thick, leather-bound books and withstand hundreds of years of scrutiny. The words were inspired by God and transcribed by ordinary men, and then later combined in an effort to understand the life of Christ.

The Gospels consist of four books: Matthew, Mark, Luke, and John. But these guys may not be who you think they are. Don't shoot the messenger. First the nativity and now this. I am probably single-handedly dismantling the things you've always believed.

Do you imagine Jesus, Matthew, Mark, Luke, and John just walking around together, watching people be healed, eating dinner together, and things like that? I mean, it's just Him and a bunch of His disciples living their best lives. These four guys must have been close, right? They're battling storms and seeing Jesus after He was raised from the dead. It's just good that they had each other.

Well, not really. So here we go. Don't say I didn't warn you.

　＊Read Luke 1:1-4 again. (We read it earlier this week.)

If that didn't set off any alarms, let me be clear: it is very likely that Luke never met Jesus. The account he wrote was based on what he had learned from eyewitnesses. He was obviously not one of the twelve disciples, as you may have figured out.[8]

And Mark? He wasn't an eyewitness either. Most scholars believe Simon Peter, one of the twelve, was his source for information on Jesus.[9]

Soooooooooo now you understand the four Gospel writers weren't all sitting around Jesus at the same time taking notes, thinking, "Wow!

Won't this make a great story someday!" Now that we've gotten that out of the way, let's talk about what they wrote.

* Open your Bibles to Matthew 1:1-17. I'm just asking you to look at it, not to read it.

Matthew kicks off his Gospel with an EXTENSIVE list of Christ's genealogy.

* Now, look over the first few verses of Mark, Luke, and John. How does each writer begin his Gospel?

* Matthew: Genealogy of Jesus

* Mark:

* Luke:

* John:

Fairly different ways to start out telling the same story, right? But why?

Don't worry, pet. I have all of the answers. Either that or I have several very large books written by very dead people who were very smart when they were alive, and I'm just repeating what they said.

The first three Gospels are called the Synoptic Gospels because they are all basically talking about the same events in Christ's life but told in different ways.[11] John is more of a poet and tells his version of the story through the lens of a creative writer. You'll never guess who my favorite is.

*The word "synoptic" means "with the same eye."[10]*

Let's start with Matthew, even though Mark wrote his account before Matthew did.[12] I didn't put them in order, so don't blame me if that's confusing. It's also important for you to know that although Matthew was one of Christ's disciples, he didn't write his account until decades after Jesus died. The exact dates are a little muddy, but the point is that it was a good while after Jesus' death.

The important thing to know about Matthew is that he is a Jew who was writing to other Jews.

*Think ALL the way back to when we talked about the man considered to be the father of the Jews. Remember? Who was it?*

If you don't remember, you're in luck because I'm about to tell you. It was Abraham.

*Now read Matthew 1:1 in light of that.*

In Old Testament prophecies, God told the Jews that the Messiah would come from Abraham and David's family line. Matthew knew that his audience would be interested in the way the "so-called Messiah" could be traced back to Abraham, so that's what Matthew does.[13]

Speaking of what Matthew does, he is a tax collector. I hope you remember how people felt about these guys. Despite that fact, he was obviously a meticulous record-keeper, which shows in his writing.

*Read Luke 5:27-28. Where was Matthew when Jesus called him to be a disciple? (Levi is another name for Matthew.)*

Matthew has, by far, the most Old Testament quotations of the four Gospels.[14]

*Here's a guy who was knee-deep in his sinful behavior, and Jesus calls him to be a follower. Why do you think Jesus chose Matthew?*

It's not certain, but some think Mark identified himself in Mark 14:51-52. If so, how embarrassing!

*Read Luke 5:29-32. Who did Jesus come for?*

Good job. And now let's take a look at Mark. He's writing about similar stories from Jesus' life, although he's not interested in the birth and childhood information. He jumps in full-force, emphasizing the miracles of Christ. He is writing to Gentile Christians, specifically the Romans, so maybe he wants to make sure they are impressed with Jesus and His power. Because remember how much the Romans love power? Yes. Good angle, Mark.

Remember, Mark isn't one of the twelve disciples, but it's pretty obvious from the way he presents his ideas that he was very influenced by Peter, who was (DING DING, CORRECT) a disciple. We're going to chat some about the disciples tomorrow, but I just want you to get a feel for the background of the Gospels themselves before we meet the characters.

Because no one in their right mind would start a puzzle without doing the edges first.

Mark likes to keep things moving—he includes the word "straightway" (or "immediately") more than forty times in his writing.[15] He's not as concerned about the fluffy stuff; he just wants to present the facts.

Next up: Dr. Luke.

You can definitely tell that he's a doctor because he talks a lot about the birth of Christ, healing, and so on. Evidently he really loves to do research. He uses great detail to make sure he's presenting an accurate account of the way things happened. As we said earlier, he wrote his Gospel account for his friend Theophilus, who was probably a Gentile Christian.[16]

*Luke is the only Gospel author who isn't Jewish. So what would he be called?*

And now we come to my precious John. It's not just me who loves Him.

*Read John 13:23. How did John describe himself?*

John's Gospel is unique. I think Matthew Henry summarizes the Gospel of John best: "He gives us more of the mystery of what the other Evangelists gave us only the history ... "[17]

Let's lean in for a minute and listen to the way he begins his writing. (P. S. John is writing to all who believe.)

*Pop over to the very beginning of John and read verses 1:1-18. How does the beginning of John's Gospel differ from the other three?*

*John is going to focus more on the deity of Jesus, rather than His humanity. How do you see that in his opening words?

*I know there's a lot of information in these eighteen verses, and it probably isn't all crystal clear. But what verses stand out to you and why?

*Are there things you understand better now than you would have a couple of weeks ago? Explain.

*Before we close today, let's pause for a moment to consider verse 14. Write it out below.

All of the Gospels tell us the same story although John is the only one who says it explicitly: "the Word became flesh and dwelt among us." Or as The Message paraphrases it: "The Word became flesh and blood, and moved into the neighborhood."

It's the heart of the entire story, and my eyes get teary when I think about what that means for me.

And what that means for you.

DAY 4

# DISCIPLES

We've all heard the phrase, "There was just something about him."

That doesn't necessarily indicate that the person is particularly beautiful, intelligent, wealthy, or powerful. But there is something that sets that person apart. Something endearing about him. Something that just draws you in.

It is not a phrase that would have been used for Moses, I'll tell you that. I don't get the feeling that he's personable or endearing. We don't see Moses having any "actual warm conversations" with people. In fact, he doesn't have many one-on-one conversations with people at all.

Most of the Torah consists of Moses and God talking. Essentially, Moses was a messenger, chosen by God to lead His people out of Egypt. Moses isn't asking anyone what their favorite manna-topper is. He's just doing his job.

In a way, he's the Old Testament summed up in one human: here's the law. Do it. If you obey, you'll be blessed. If you don't, you'll be punished. So who wants to grab a swimsuit and head to the waterpark?

When we get to New Testament times, Jewish society still functioned in much the same way as it had for hundreds of years. The law governed life, and the Pharisees governed the laws.

It was a formal system with blatant rules. Forgiveness only comes through sacrifices and even that is temporary. I imagine life back then would be saturated by the feeling of failure and sadness; there was always an impossible standard weighing down on them.

It's easy to step back from this time period and feel no emotion about their circumstances. But if we don't enter the story, see it, understand it, apply it—then we'll miss the way Jesus loves us.

Jesus brought a new way of life, a new teaching—"You've heard it said ... but I tell you ..."

The Old Testament is forced; the new covenant is asked.

Jesus isn't demanding; He's inviting.

Sure, Jesus requires things of us as His followers, but the things He gives us to do are only for our good, to show how wonderful God is—they are never petty or unkind.

It's obvious from the very first words He uses in John's Gospel with some men who would become His disciples.

*Turn to John 1:35-42.

*What does Jesus ask them?

There is so much that could be wrapped up in this question. And you, my friend, are asked the same: "What do you want from Me?"

The teachings of Jesus reach far beyond the last pages of the Bible. They stretch out to you, exactly where you are in this moment, with the same power.

*Take a second and just write down the very first thoughts that come to your mind when you consider that question. And be honest. You might have answers that surprise you or make you realize the way you see Him. Get it down on paper and let's catch up with the disciples when you're done.

Well done.

*What did the disciples say to Him in response to His question?

It feels like a strange answer, but we'll just go with it.

*What did Jesus say in response to them?

It's like a battle of the questions. And Jesus wins. As you will see, no one can beat Him in a game of "dodge the answer." Actually no one can beat Him in a game of anything, but this particular area is unparalleled.

*What term do the men use to address Him when they ask Him where He is staying?*

The Scripture says they spend the day with Jesus, and then Andrew heads out to find his brother Simon and tell him the good news.

*How does Andrew refer to Jesus in verse 41?*

Andrew spent a couple of hours with a complete stranger and went from calling Him a teacher to the Savior of the world.

Like I said, there must have been something about Him.

*What did Jesus tell Simon in verse 42?*

So this is why the same guy is referred to as Simon, Simon Peter, or Peter. I love when Scripture makes things easy. Also, I just love Peter.

Now listen, I told you earlier that there are different versions of stories in the Gospels, and that seems to be the case here with the calling of Andrew and Peter.

*Read Mark 1:16-20. How is this story about the calling of Simon and Andrew different from what you just read in John?*

There is definitely some variation in the way it's presented, but we have to remember that the heart of the story remains the same. He calls them by way of invitation in some form or fashion.

Let's get back to my precious Peter. Simon Pe ... never mind. You get it.

*Go to Luke 5:1-11.*

I love this one. And remember, be curious.

"Lake of Gennesaret" is another name for the Sea of Galilee. It's also called "Sea of Tiberias" (John 6:1; 21:1).

*After you read the verses, jot down anything you think stands out or makes you ask more questions.

*What are the fishermen doing (5:2)?

*Jesus hops in Simon's boat and what is the first thing He does?

**Pay attention to the way this whole thing goes down.**

*After He teaches, what does He tell Simon to do?

*What is Simon's response?

Luke is the only writer in the New Testament who uses the term "Master" for Jesus. And this term is only used by Jesus' followers. The title of "Teacher" was only used by strangers and "Rabbi" was never used in his Gospel.[18]

*What happens when he obeys?

The nets are breaking. The boats are sinking. The fish are flailing around. And you know what my favorite part is?

*BUT.*

You think I'm kidding? I just teared up reading verse 8:

> But when Simon Peter saw it, he fell down at Jesus' knees saying, "Depart from me, for I am a sinful man, O Lord."
> **LUKE 5:8**

Remember when I told you to picture yourself there? This is the perfect moment to do so.

There is MASS chaos happening. There are (presumably) hundreds of people there, all desperate to see and hear this man named Jesus. He instructs the fishermen to do something that seems ridiculous, and now everyone is watching to see what will happen next.

> * And when the impossible happens, what do the fisherman do?

JESUS' TWELVE
DISCIPLES

---

Andrew
Bartholomew
James,
the son of Alphaeus
James,
the son of Zebedee
John
Judas Iscariot
Matthew
(Simon) Peter
Philip
Simon, the Zealot
Thaddaeus
Thomas

(See Matt. 10:2-4.)

Like, I know they need some fish for their business, but I'm just wondering why they didn't jump out of their boats and freak out.

Well, I can tell you why: I mean, it's a theory, but go with me. I think they wanted the gift more than they wanted the Giver.

All except for one—one guy whose life will tell a wild and precious tale.

Compare Jesus' words with the Old Testament teaching. Same God. Same character. Different covenant.

He teaches. He invites them to listen and obey. He shows evidence of His power. He allows the people to make their own decisions based on what they have seen and heard.

There are four words I love in verse ten—maybe you can take a guess about what they are.

Ten dollars (that you will never get) says you're wrong. Although I do think Jesus telling Simon not to be afraid was important, it's the next part where I get a little misty: *Jesus said to Simon.*

He's not talking to the crowd, regardless of how you've read it in the past.

He's speaking to the one who realized that you can't truly appreciate a gift until you can comprehend how little you deserve it.

DAY 5
# NICODEMUS

It was somewhere around this point when I realized that I had made a terrible decision about a Bible study topic.

Don't get me wrong. I love Jesus, and I love teaching about Him. But the idea of writing a study on His entire life—all of the teaching, all of the miracles, all of the details of His travels and relationships with people on earth and His Father in heaven, the Passion Week, and on and on and on. The deeper I get into the text, the more I want to write about. But teaching on one story means there won't be room for this other great story or the intricate details He has woven into every corner of His existence. It's quite a conundrum.

\* *Read John 21:25. What was John's proclamation?*

Choose Your Own Adventure® is a series of children's books written from the second-person point of view where the reader chooses the main character's actions and story outcome.[19]

You'd think I would have considered these points before I eagerly signed a contract, but no. I did not. So here we are. Did you ever read those Choose Your Own Adventure® books? I would love to give you options for where you go next. Those of you who want to skip past the details and just get the facts should take path one. If you like to focus on one story and look for the original Greek words and Google®, "What does a fig tree represent?" I'm going to recommend path two. Don't go on path three because that's the one where you find out you died.

The truth is that I can't do both, so I have decided to use the rest of my time with you analyzing *Dateline*® episodes instead. I have never missed a single one, and I promise you if my husband ever does me wrong you will never find the body.

How do you paint a picture that has a background and the subject matter? I guess I'm not exactly sure, but I'm going to try. What I have asked of the Lord is the opportunity to sit with you and give you enough of Jesus' story to make you hungry for the rest. I'm kind of the appetizer, you know?

We know Jesus spent a lot of His ministry with people around Him. The Bible tells us Jesus was moved with compassion, He *saw* people in those settings, He met their needs—both the spiritual and the physical.

*Read Mark 6:34 and 8:1-10. Note how Jesus ministered to the crowds.*

But the heart of Jesus' ministry was not about feeding the faceless crowds.

He chose a tax collector, an honest Israelite, and a backwater fisherman. He saw the one—the individual.

*Find the story of Nicodemus in John 3:1-15. Go ahead and read it but don't be overwhelmed by it quite yet; we're going to break this baby down.*

*For starters, how is Nicodemus described in verse 1?*

We've got your number, Nic.

*He travels by night to see Jesus, which may or may not be because he was afraid of being seen by other Pharisees. Regardless, what does he say to Jesus in verse 2?*

*Write down Jesus' response to him (v. 3).*

Jesus' words are obviously a bit perplexing to Nicodemus. He is a wee bit concerned that re-entering his mother's womb is, well, UNLIKELY.

But here's the point: Nicodemus is earnest in wanting to know what it means to be "born again."

*Jesus tells him that unless he is born of* _____ *and* _____, *he cannot enter the* _____ _____ _____ *(v. 5).*

Nicodemus seems particularly confused about the fact that something might be required of him in order to have eternal security. He thought he was already "in" as part of God's chosen people and one who follows God's law.

I would imagine that as a Pharisee, Nicodemus is mostly concerned with doing things in order to be righteous, but take note of what Jesus is saying. You must be *born again* in order to be with Him. You don't get into the kingdom because of what you do, but by something done for you.

Remember that time you birthed yourself?

Or were you born without any effort of your own?

Jesus alludes to His death in verse 14, and then He goes on to speak the most quoted verses in Scripture.

According to Bible Gateway, John 3:16 is the most read Bible verse. In case you're wondering, Jeremiah 29:11 comes in second.[20]

* *Read verses 16-18. What do we have to do in order to have eternal life?*

* *How would you summarize verses 17-18?*

God sent His Son to the world—not to condemn the world, but to save it.

He came so that all the people in the world would know God. The veiled inference in this explanation is that it makes no difference if you are a Jew or a Gentile, those who believe will be saved.

I don't know which version of the Bible you're using, but flip to Isaiah 49:6b. My version says, "I will make you as a light for the nations, that my salvation may reach to the end of the earth." I want to mention that the original text doesn't just say "for the nations." It specifically says "Gentiles"—*a light for the Gentiles.*

What Jesus is telling Nicodemus is that this isn't a transaction based on behavior (as he has believed). It is the desire for relationship based on love. You don't do it; you accept it.

*It's a proposal.*

We don't get to see Nicodemus' response here. But at some point, it seems, he understands.

Other Scriptures show us that Nicodemus answers in a way similar to the way Mary did: *I believe you, but I don't understand how this happens.*

* Read John 19:38-42. What do we find out about Nicodemus in this passage?

What this powerful, religious, respected leader has begun to understand is that the only way he can gain Christ is to lose the world he has known.

Jesus is abundantly clear: following Me is not easy. You will be hated, persecuted, and targeted by the enemy. You will have to deny yourself and pick up your cross.

And everyone knows that you only carry a cross for one reason: to be crucified on. You aren't coming back. You die to self. To your old life.

We cannot deserve the gift He has offered to us. We're incapable of such a thing.

The only thing we can do is run to Him, confess how unworthy we are, and ask for His forgiveness. If that's something you've never done, there is more information on page 207 that will walk you through it more thoroughly. Regardless, I can't wait to see you back here next week.

Jesus is no ordinary Teacher, that's for sure.

Put your student hat on, grab a canteen of water, and make sure you've got your old Birkenstocks®. We're headed wherever He's going, soaking up every bit of teaching we can as we go.

*Rabbi, we know that You are a Teacher come from God.*

four

WEEK 4

# PURPOSE: THE TEACHER

When someone uses the word *teacher*, I'm instantly transported back to sitting in the last row of Spanish class drawing mustaches on the women in my textbook.

Or I've landed back in history class where the British girl was teacher's pet. On that particular day, she was wearing some kind of weird getup, and then our teacher announced that she had memorized a monologue related to a war or some other historical event that I missed because Mrs. Ennison, while extremely knowledgeable and passionate about the subject, had not figured out a way to change her voice tone. It was the class before lunch, so the odds were already stacked against her. Or I think about the time my sixth grade math teacher said, "If you can answer all of these correctly, you will not have homework. But—and this is a BIG BUT—if you don't …"

It was too late. We were already giggling in that way that means it's not going to stop until after the bell rings.

I also think about my college English professor handing back our papers after writing on the board the number of As, Bs, Cs, and so on. One A in the whole class. I hung my head. I had written about my dad, and I had actually cared about the way it turned out. When my paper landed on my desk, I flipped it over and saw "97%" and almost started crying. Do you want to know something crazy? It was such a defining moment in my life that I can still quote the last line: "With the audience on its feet and the world in the palm of my hand, I smiled victoriously."

Our teachers shape the way we understand the subject, but they also shape the way we experience it.

There's no question that Jesus is the best teacher who has ever lived. I'm pretty sure the fact that the New Testament exists is good evidence that people were paying attention and taking in every word He said.

They also had the privilege of seeing firsthand what we can only see on pages; He taught by living it out in a way that stuck with them. He didn't just inform them—He showed them.

In other words, I doubt the disciples ever had to resort to mustaches or monologues.

## GROUP SESSION GUIDE

### SESSION 4: REVIEW WEEK 3 HOMEWORK.

* What new things did you grasp from the Scripture this week in your homework?

* Day 1: Who was John the Baptist? Why does the Bible say he was put on earth?

* Consider your relationship with Jesus. Do you point people to Jesus naturally? Or is it harder for you?

* Day 2: Jesus was tempted in His humanity in much the same way that we are, but He never gave in. He never sinned. Does this truth make you feel more understood by Jesus? Or do you feel inferior? Does your reaction say something about the way you view God?

* Day 3: Which Gospel writer appeals to your learning style more? Dr. Luke? Tax collector Matthew? Tell your group what about that specific writer and Gospel account stands out to you.

* Day 4: Jesus doesn't demand that we follow Him, He invites us to follow Him. What's the difference? How have you experienced it?

* Day 5: Who was Nicodemus? What did Jesus tell him about faith? Why was it so strange to hear?

**WATCH SESSION 4 (VIDEO RUN TIME: 8:12)**

## DISCUSS

* What part of the video spoke to you the most? Why?

* Do you find yourself striving to understand all about God instead of trying to understand God? Unpack the difference between the two and why one is easier for you.

* Love is more important than knowledge. Name a few ways that you struggle to put relationship over knowledge.

* Do you tend to compare yourself to the rest of the pew or ask Jesus if you're living the way He'd like you to? Explain your answer to your group.

* Are you brave enough to trust Jesus to love you even when you get it wrong? Why or why not?

Video sessions available for purchase or rent
at *LifeWay.com/Matchless*

DAY 1
# THE REASON HE CAME

Today we are going to list all of the reasons Jesus came to earth.

That is inaccurate and misleading, but we are going to cover quite a bit, so I hope you've brought your coffee and curiosity.

*If someone were to ask you why Jesus came to the earth, what would you say?*

I really want to know what you wrote. Maybe you can email me.

There are many, many, many good answers, and that's kind of the point of today's work. Typically we answer those kinds of questions with a good one-liner that sums up the most extraordinary thing Jesus did: He was crucified on our behalf and resurrected in order to give us new life.

There are a lot of variations of that answer, but it's probably pretty close to yours. One thousand percent true, but not the full answer.

Jesus didn't *just* come to the world to die for us; He came to live with us.

The best way to approach today's work is by rapid-fire. So—here you go: these concepts might not make complete sense at this point, but they will. I want you to jump into the rest of this week with them in your mind. Perfect.

1. Jesus came to experience life as a human.
2. Jesus came to seek and save the lost.
3. Jesus redefined "the lost" and came to teach what true salvation is.
4. Jesus came to fulfill the Law of Moses.
5. Jesus came to tell us about the kingdom of God.
6. Jesus came to model life with God.
7. Jesus came to fulfill prophecy.
8. Jesus came to be our Passover Lamb.
9. Jesus came with power and performed miracles only the Messiah could.
10. Jesus came to show us His love in a way we could identify with.

You don't have to memorize those, and there won't be a quiz—at least not today.

He was born to a normal woman in an unremarkable way, and yet the traces of prophecy are braided throughout the story in an undeniable way. From the beginning of His life on earth to the end, Jesus lived a life that fully and perfectly fulfilled the description of the coming Messiah.

 * *Let's kick this off with John 8:31-37. Who is He speaking to?*

 * *What does He say is required in order to be a true disciple?*

Up until now, the Jews had been pretty confident of where they stood with God because they were descendants of Abraham, part of God's chosen people. Jesus' statement is radical because He is basically telling the Jews that they can't just get by based solely on their place in God's family tree. God requires personal obedience from the heart to be a true disciple.

Jesus' teaching here bypasses the fact that Jews and Gentiles are completely different classes of people. His words are essentially telling them that it isn't going to be this way anymore.

 * *But who is Jesus ultimately talking to when He explains what's required in order to be a disciple?*

I'll give you a clue: the answer is *everybody*. Including you.

*If you love me, you will keep my commandments.*
**JOHN 14:15**

Full stop.

Here's something I want you to commit to doing for the rest of this study: don't walk away from any passages feeling stupid because there were things you didn't understand. Think about how much you did understand and be encouraged. Also, you may run across people in life who want to make sure you can spell all the names in the Old Testament and quote every word Jesus uttered and are more than happy to use that as evidence of intelligence.

Instead of trying to teach you the specifics of every time Jesus teaches, performs miracles, or models life with His Father, I'm going to focus on certain moments in His life that show us *who* He was teaching, *how* He taught, and *why* He did it the way He did. That way, you'll have a firm biblical foundation as you read Scripture on your own, and it'll set you up to interpret all of the things we can't cover in this study.

We see people like this in the Bible. They're referred to as Pharisees; and, as you're going to see, these are not your people. Jesus had a lot of the same opinions about them btw, so you're in good company. When you're asked to read Scripture in this study:

- ❏ *Read all of it.*
- ❏ *Recognize what you understand (even in a small sense).*
- ❏ *Reframe your approach and decide to be curious but not self-condemning.*
- ❏ *Resist the urge to think you aren't smart enough to understand the text.*
- ❏ *Remember to ask questions.*
- ❏ *Remind yourself that He wrote this for you.*
- ❏ *Accept that I love alliteration.*
- ❏ *Anticipate the fact that I will continue to use it.*

In the past few weeks, you've worked your tail off to understand some of the context and background of Jesus' life. Now, I want you to read John 1:1-18 because it'll summarize a lot of what you've studied, and hopefully, you'll be glad you did all that work. *(We've read this passage before, but it's important for our study today too.)* Then, we're going to do a quick run-through of the list above.

\* *What questions can you ask of the text?*

I'll go ahead and answer that one, because I'm already a little confused by verses 1-2. How did the Word live? How could this Word live with God and also be God?

It's really easy to read something like this and pull out a quote that sounds familiar or important. "In the beginning was the Word." Love it. Quote it. Tell Janet you love the fact that she has it on her key chain.

Can I be honest? Again, I realize I'm not your typical Bible teacher, but I'm going to level with you. I'm still a little confused about it. I'm going to be straightforward about my follow-up thought as well—Jesus does not and will never hold that against me. There is a deliberate mystery He has chosen to impart alongside His Word. I think it's easy to hold our-less-than-perfect-ability to understand against ourselves and assume we are terrible Christians rather than recognize that salvation is not reliant on how quickly we raise our hands.

It's not about the answers; it's about the heart. It isn't keeping the Law out of obligation that matters—it's obedience that pours from a true love of Christ.

I assure you that God will not decide whether or not to welcome you into heaven based on how you score on a Bible knowledge quiz or how many times you kept Sabbath.

Are you ready for this? God knew we would never be able to keep the commandments perfectly. He knew we would try to offer something in order to cover our sin temporarily. He knew the point of the law was to show everyone how much they needed a Savior, not to score their exams.

> \*Thinking about everything we've just discussed regarding God's grace and how He knows we're not perfect, do you feel relief? Anxiety? Explain.

As it says in John 1:17: "For the law was given through Moses; grace and truth came through Jesus Christ." Jesus came as the better Moses: the One who would lead His people to the land He has always promised them and who would rescue them from spiritual slavery instead of physical slavery. He would point to the Old Testament and Moses, not as a framework for salvation but as a text He knew was familiar to them.

For more on Jesus as the better and greater Moses, see Hebrews 3.

The truth will set you free.

If you want to be set free, you have to understand the truth.

Word made flesh.

I may not be able to explain it perfectly with my mouth, but my heart believes it irrefutably.

Tomorrow we're going to show up as students sitting under the greatest Teacher who ever lived, and we're going to listen in ways we never have before.

DAY 2
# IT'S ABOUT THE HEART

I think it's clear by now that Jesus was an amazing teacher.

This week we're going to talk about the methods Jesus used to teach while He was on earth.

You've probably heard that He tells a lot of stories (usually parables—we'll talk about that later) and asks a lot of questions. That's true. But I think a better way to study His teaching is to become His student instead of making flashcards.

So we walk into His classroom. (Which, incidentally, tends to be a hillside or some other random place. He isn't really a "class is from 7–4 on Mt. Sinai" kind of Teacher.) So I guess it's better to say we're walking *with* His classroom.

And here's your challenge: as we read through the next several days, put your name in the text. Don't worry. I'll remind you.

There's a common pattern Jesus uses to teach the people around Him. (Yes, you can start seeing yourself in the crowd.)

He begins by acknowledging a concept that was familiar to His audience in some way. He makes a connection. It may be by going to their turf or using fishing terms for fishermen and farming terms with farmers.

Time and time again when Jesus opens His mouth, it seems His ultimate goal is to unpack the true meaning of the law they are living under.

He *acknowledges* their belief system in order to *challenge* it, *explain* it, *model* it, and *invite* people to believe in Him as their Savior.

*Hop on over to Matthew 5 and read verse 1.

This is called the Sermon on the Mount because, well, Jesus is sitting on a mountain. You may also recall that Moses was on a mountain when he received the Ten Commandments. Coincidence? I think not.

Jesus delivers the longest discourse of His lifetime here, and it includes enough information to write one hundred Bible studies and still not feel like you've covered much ground.

*He starts out with the Beatitudes, which are nine
statements regarding who will be considered blessed.
Let's dig in here for a second. It'll be worth it; I promise.

1. Blessed are _____,
   for theirs _____.

2. Blessed are _____,
   for they _____.

3. Blessed are _____,
   for they _____.

4. Blessed are _____,
   for they _____.

5. Blessed are _____,
   for they _____.

6. Blessed are _____,
   for they _____.

7. Blessed are _____,
   for they _____.

8. Blessed are _____,
   for theirs _____.

9. Blessed are _____,
   for _____.

> **Beatitude** comes from the Latin word *beatus*, which means "blessings."

That last one packs a punch, doesn't it? Look at the words He is using to describe the way His followers should be.

Well, He came in like a wrecking ball on that one, didn't He?

I mean, THIS SOUNDS LIKE THE LIFE I HAVE DREAMED OF.

This is not by accident, in case you were wondering. Jesus knows this would shock those who are listening because it is counterintuitive for them to think a Messiah would want them to be meek and hungry. He is telling them right off the bat that He is not the warrior King they had thought (and hoped) He would be.

If you were to skim over the Sermon on the Mount, you would no doubt see a lot of embroidery/Etsy® inspiration. For example: Love your enemies. You are the salt of the earth. Don't be anxious. Ask and it will be given. The golden rule and on and on and on.

It's sort of the Greatest Hits album of His ministry.

  * But now we're going to zoom in a little. Read Matthew 5:17.

   "Do not think that I have come to _____ the Law
   or the Prophets; I have not come to _____
   them but to _____ them."

This is one of the most important sentences that Christ issued during His lifetime. Really.

Jesus is telling His disciples that He isn't getting rid of the Ten Commandments, but He is explaining their truest meaning in order for people to understand the *spirit* of the law and simply not the *letter* of the law.

This is important because if He had busted onto the scene telling them that the Ten Commandments never existed and the prophets of the Old Testament were just a bunch of nutty guys who made up stories, He would have been written off as a blasphemer before He taught His first lesson.

But He doesn't, which is why it was so tricky for His enemies to pin Him down.

Think about this: your Teacher is a Jewish man. He is a man who knows the Old Testament better than any scribe or Pharisee ever could. How do you condemn a man who appears to be your superior in knowledge and is well-loved by His many followers?

  * Go to Matthew 5:21 and then 27,33,38—you get the point.
   What is the repeated phrase?

Jesus is telling them that He knows the law, and He also knows the way it has been twisted and used in ways it was never meant to be.

And here's the kicker: He's not really loosening up on the important rules; He is actually tightening the reins.

> *Read Matthew 5:27-28. How did Jesus tighten the reins here?*

Does it sound like He's removing that law? Um, no. He just made it about ten million times harder.

Now it isn't just about the outward behavior, it's about the inward motive.

And there is no place in Scripture where He says it's going to be easy. In fact, He says that it will be hard—that we will have to die to ourselves, carry our crosses, and expect to be persecuted and despised.

WHERE DO I SIGN UP????

I know. It's an odd marketing strategy. And if that were the end of the story, I would probably be a forensic psychologist who moonlights as a *Dateline* anchor.

Drumroll: it isn't.

I told you that you were going to have a front row seat as Jesus taught, so I'm going to ask you a question (even though I have complete confidence that your answers will look like mine and like everyone around you).

> *Are there times when you focus on other people's behavior without considering their motive or internal thinking?*

*Do you ever emphasize your own behavior and use it as a litmus test for your faith? Give a couple examples.*

Janet, I *acknowledge* your empty lines and your commitment to not committing.

Here's the thing—if you don't believe you've ever put behavior on top of the list, you need to go back to that list of commandments. The one about lying is still in full force.

More times than not, our knee-jerk reaction is to *do*, and it's no different with our faith.

*How does our faith become about doing rather than being? How does this hinder our relationship with Christ?*

Ultimately, it boils down to wanting control, which is a concept I hear is common in the general public.

Actually, there is a story about me as a toddler that will live in infamy. When I was eighteen months old and stuffed in a clown costume on Halloween, I refused to let anyone else hand out the candy. I stood at the door clutching the pumpkin basket and pushing away anyone who came near me while screaming, "ME DO!" over and over.

I can't tell you how many times my family and friends have repeated that phrase to me in my life when I'm being stubborn or determined to do things myself.

I always seem to find spiritual lessons in everyday life, which is why I immediately thought of the way I remodeled my dad's house after he passed away. I had an inkling of how much physical pain and emotional suffering would be involved: and yes, I was mocked for trying. (You know who you are. I accept your apology and offer you a bite-sized Snickers® bar as a sign of my forgiveness.)

To be clear, I ended up in the ER with a concussion caused by accidentally hitting myself in the head with a hammer. Don't ask. (I had to explain it

to the contractors the next day because it looked a little like a crime scene.) I was electrocuted. I fell off a ladder. The list goes on and on.

The truth is that we make a decision to walk into something that requires sacrifice and commitment without knowing exactly what it's going to be like at the end.

In the smallest of ways, I felt that while I worked. What's the point? Just give up and walk away. Let someone else do it.

I am smiling as I write this, because I know the answer: It looked like redemption when it was finished.

I think my dad would have been proud of me. He probably would have been laughing and whispering, "Me do. Me do."

And he probably would have gotten a kick out of the fact that I left a large pumpkin basket full of candy right by the door for anyone who came to the house.

My dad taught me the best lessons of my life by simply living them out.

But it wasn't the hugs, and it wasn't the way he laughed at my jokes. It wasn't the fact that he cut articles out of the newspaper that he thought I might like or that he never missed a single game that I cheered at. (Nor did he miss one of my soccer games when I was on a team called the Brown Bombers. You know how teams can be undefeated in a season? Yeah. We were defeated.)

It wasn't the letters he wrote to me when I went away to college—they're more poetic than I could ever dream of writing. Those were beautiful actions, but it was his intentions that convinced me I was loved.

I knew where those moments were created before they reached me.

When your Father looks at you, He sees His beloved child. And everything He does is an overflow of a love we can't begin to understand.

It wasn't the mountain, and it wasn't the beams of wood. It wasn't the cave in Nazareth or the miracles.

It was the fact that His eyes were steadied on you the whole time.

I don't know if your dad helped you love Jesus or if he made it hard to believe God was real. I pray it's the former, but in either case, hear me say this and fasten it to your heart:

*He thought you were worth all of it, and where you see brokenness, He sees redemption.*

Blessed are those who believe it.

DAY 3

# CHALLENGING THE MOTIVATION

Welcome back! Today we're going to talk some more about the way Jesus taught, and again, the emphasis is on connecting His teaching to the Old Testament and learning how we are called to live in the present day.

Let me say this: Jesus knows how to stir people up, and He is not afraid to do so. He makes people furious, and He challenges every bit of their broken theology.

He is always, always pushing people to question themselves and their motives instead of rebuking them in superficial ways. And it's fun to pretend you're there in person watching these situations go down, because more often than not, they end with people who have been stunned silent. Even the top dogs were left with no way around His words.

Jesus has met them in the place where they are, living under the burden of the law, and that's where He's going to challenge them.

The fourth commandment tells us that we must take a Sabbath day; technically it says to "remember the Sabbath day, to keep it holy" (Ex. 20:8). I am all for this. And so were they. The religious leaders decided it would be better to make the idea of Sabbath a little more detailed. Why not? Laws are fun.

   *Read the words of Moses as he passed down the
   commandment in Deuteronomy 5:12-15.

   *OK—so on the seventh day, what are we supposed to
   refrain from doing?

In addition, your donkey and male servants need to take it easy as well.

The basic explanation of the commandment as it was handed down from God is simply, "Do not work."

You wouldn't believe how far the Pharisees took that one. You weren't allowed to put in false teeth because it was considered work.[1]

They also made a rule that you couldn't look in a mirror because you might be tempted to pull out a gray hair, which would also be considered a violation of the law.[2]

Also, don't even THINK about rearranging your bedroom. You aren't allowed to move furniture on the Sabbath.[3] The good news is that you're allowed to take out a ladder, but you can't move it more than four steps.[4]

This next one might be my favorite because the level of "out of the box thinking" is at an ALL-TIME HIGH.

You are permitted to spit on a rock during the Sabbath, but not on the ground. It could make mud, which would be considered mortar—which would be considered work.[5]

If you're having a restless night, Google this stuff. Don't even get me started about the radish-eating rule.[6]

I hope you are tracking with me: God gave Moses the commandments, and over time the religious leaders added the oral law. Their intention was good; they wanted to help the people follow the law more easily. But instead, it burdened the people—which is just another way of reminding us that we can never keep the law no matter how perfectly we try. Look back at our explanation on page 45.

\* *Turn to John 5:1 and read through verse 9.*

This is one of those stories that I have always been fascinated by because the question Jesus asks seems so ridiculous. *Do I want to get well? I've been in this condition for thirty-eight years. What do you think?*

But that isn't what he said. He didn't even answer the question.

\* *What was his response (v. 7)?*

Verses 3b-4 are left out of most modern translations because they are not found in the earliest and most reliable Greek texts and the language used is foreign to John's writing. It's thought these words were added later.[7]

You see, there was this idea about the pool of Bethesda. People said angels occasionally stirred up the water in the pool, and it was first-come, first-heal at that point. And this guy is complaining that no one would bring him down. Hmm. That's interesting.

Maybe he had given up on healing. Or maybe he didn't want to be healed—after all, this was his livelihood. Being a beggar was what kept his cash flow coming. It isn't like *beggar* looks good on a resume. But then Jesus shows up to this place where there were likely many beggars, and He walks directly to this particular man. Despite the fact that the beggar never said *yes* to Jesus' offer, Jesus takes matters into His own hands.

* *What does Jesus tell the disabled man to do, and what does the man do in response?*

I don't think there's any question about whether or not a lame and blind man being healed after thirty-eight years is a miracle.

Here's why I can't rush through Scripture: I feel like we didn't get enough information. Now I want to know what the man felt when he was healed and whether or not he thanked Jesus. Or why Jesus told him to pick up his mat instead of just telling him to get up and walk.

* *Turns out, the last question is about to be answered. Read verses 10-13 and feel free to laugh at what is happening.*

A man who hasn't walked in thirty-eight years and is now able to stand and move is being criticized for PICKING UP HIS MAT on the Sabbath.

How dare he. I mean, I think we can acknowledge the fact that there were other options. For example: "Heyyyyyyy, man. I really want to celebrate the fact that you've been inexplicably healed. We should def throw a party. I don't know what kind of handmade crafts we make for this kind of thing, but I guarantee Pinterest® does! On it."

I mean, the guy was *this close* to a hallelujah party, but unfortunately he picked up his mat. His first spin of the wheel earned him ninety cents, and he decided to spin again. When the needle bareelllyyyy made it to fifteen cents, the studio audience gave a synchronized groan on his behalf.

Let's go back to the actual event. Now can you see why Jesus included this little "pick up your mat" tidbit? Because Jesus knew that, to the religious leaders, the law would trump anything else, including miraculous healing.

Dissect that a teensy bit more: in their eyes, obedience to the specific command given by God Himself is still subservient to their man-made laws.

＊A similar incident occurred in Mark 2:1-12. Read it and write down what happened.

You probably noticed a couple of differences between this story and our miracle at the pool story in John 5. First, this one wasn't on the Sabbath. And this time, the man was brought by his friends, who were practically begging for Jesus to heal him.

Isn't it interesting that neither of these men ever asked to be healed? Jesus doesn't need them to. His will remains His will and is not dependent on man's behavior. Oh wait, that sounds familiar.

＊What are the scribes upset about before Jesus physically heals the man?

＊What does Jesus ask them?

There's no question we would all answer the way I'm convinced they did in their minds; of course, physical healing seems more miraculous. Why? *Because we can see evidence of it.*

I imagine Jesus looking at them, His gaze steady and His voice calm.

"Rise, pick up your bed, and go home." And everyone present watches in astonishment as the paralyzed man does exactly that. It was more than a party trick, though—Jesus is showing His authority over both the physical and spiritual worlds.

Not only can He heal our bodies, but more importantly, He can forgive our sins.

＊Head over to Isaiah 29:13. But before you do that, just a quick quiz:

The Book of Isaiah is in the _____ Testament.
The man Isaiah was a _____, and his basic job description was to _____.

I'm beaming with pride. You are my favorite students of all time.

✳ *Write out Isaiah 29:13:*

Hmm—that sounds like a pretty accurate prophecy, but let's be sure.

✳ *Turn to Mark and read verses 7:1-13.*

## CORBAN

The word actually means "an offering or gift dedicated to God." So if someone said the word "corban" over their money or goods, those resources could not be given to anyone, even their parents. But, here's the deal, the stuff they had dedicated to God could still be used for their own personal gain or enjoyment.[8]

I still don't really know what all the Corban part is about. (I've included a little extra info about it in the sidebar for you, in case you love facts too.) But, remember, right now we are painting the background and gathering paint colors. We don't need to spend too much time worrying about the final touches right this second.

The scribes and Pharisees are so determined to prove Jesus is a sinner that they miss the craziest part of what He's saying: you guys are the ones He was talking about. You're the stars of this play, folks.

They know Scripture. They're the ones who teach it to everyone else.

But they can't live out what they don't understand.

I would daresay many of us aren't that different.

So despite the fact that there are a lot of solid one-liners in this part of Scripture, I have decided that my favorite verse in this section of Scripture is Mark 7:8.

> *Abandoning the command of God, you*
> *hold on to human tradition.*
> **MARK 7:8, CSB**

I guess it's because I never fully understood the gravity of His words or the way they applied to me as well as the Pharisees and teachers. With that said, I am not predicting a surge in T-shirt sales with that verse on the back. Have no fear: we've got the one about Corban waiting in the wings.

Incidentally, do you ever feel sorry for the emojis that never get used on your phone? Who uses the mermaid guy or the crane picking up a block? What about the green guy with the masquerade mask? Did you even know they existed? Exactly. And you and I both know they hate running into the tears-straight-down-the-face guy or the blowing-kiss one. Guarantee those guys get to have lunch with the laughing-so-hard-I'm-crying guy and his brother the one-eye-wink fella.

Poor Corban. He'll never be a 1 Corinthians 13:4-7 guy.

But listen: don't miss the beauty of what Jesus is saying here. He's effortlessly quoting Scripture they know, upholding the law they're trying to prove He's against, rebuking them for missing the point, and quoting Moses within about three verses.

He ends the lesson with a bang, saying: You have made "void the word of God by your tradition you have handed down" (Mark 7:13a).

I really wish I could see a leper hiding in the background as he mouths, "Oooooooooo …. bussssteddd …"

They missed the point. *Are we?*

They cannot seem to grasp the notion that the inside could possibly be as important as the outside. The caste system they have created is beginning to crumble and that's not ideal.

But Jesus came to flip the script.

His chosen people hadn't chosen Him in the past, and they are clearly sticking with that pattern even when He is standing in front of them.

They are no less in need than the beggars and the blind they have walked past for years—a thought that has never occurred to them.

How could that have been? They were elite, respected, upper-class men. And that has always been enough.

*What does Jesus call them in Matthew 23:27?*

Before thousands of people descended on Israel for the Passover, all of the tombstones were painted white in order to prevent people from becoming unclean in the event that they accidentally touched one.[9]

Nothing other than their appearance changed. They are still the same broken, aging grave-markers they have always been. And up until now they have assumed that the problem could be solved without acknowledging it.

But as we know, paint can only last so long. It's a temporary fix.

Which is why the loyal children of God repainted them every year at the Passover festival—just before the temple filled with sacrificial lambs.

DAY 4

# WHO'S MY NEIGHBOR?

Jesus loved to tell stories. In fact, there isn't much of His teaching that doesn't include some aspect of storytelling.

He isn't a bullet point guy. The stories He tells are usually parables, which kind of have a funny role in Scripture. A parable is simply a story that's meant to illustrate a moral or spiritual lesson in a way that people can understand. (Or can they? We'll get there.)

And He tells A LOT OF THEM. Sometimes I think, *I would be so frustrated if I asked someone where we should go for dinner and they responded by telling me about a dog running in a field looking for his owner.*

Parables can genuinely seem that obscure.

> *Read Luke 8:9-10. What does Jesus say about the purpose of parables?*

> *What does it say in Isaiah 6:9?*

Basically, Jesus is telling us that parables help reveal the state of people's hearts toward God. Jesus tells parables in a way that requires His listeners to look more deeply to get the true intention. Some people do and some people don't.

The Jews and Gentiles have always been two separate groups of people, but Jesus begins to introduce the idea that it isn't going to be that way anymore. The split will now fall between those who believe He is Messiah and those who don't, obviously a controversial and baffling announcement.

> *Turn to Luke 10:25-37 and read through it before we get going.*

All right, so at least you have a general idea of the story. Let's pull the lens back to the bigger picture because I know you're about to ask me to tell you the story of the Jewish people and their relationship with the Samaritans.

To be honest, I just thought *Samaritan* meant a nice guy who had empathy. Turns out, I've misunderstood it from the very first day of my life when I was born at Good Samaritan Hospital in Cincinnati.

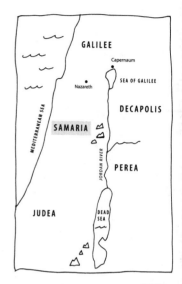

The fact that the word *good* is sitting next to the word *Samaritan* is VERY odd. Did you know that? It's true. At this point in time there would be no chance of a Jew using that phrase because they hated the Samaritans. Check out our map in the margin (or flip to the big one in the back) so we can just take a quick peek at where Samaria is so the rest of this will make a little more sense.

OK. See how easy it would be for people traveling from Judea to, say, Galilee to walk straight through Samaria? But they typically don't. They travel all the way around, going over to Perea and heading right along the Jordan River into Decapolis in order to avoid it.

You're dying to know why the Jews hate the Samaritans. I've got the answer for you. Remember in Week 1 when we talked about the Northern and Southern Kingdoms and God's people in exile? At one point, Israel (aka the Northern Kingdom) was conquered by another nation known as the Assyrians. After their victory, the Assyrians deported most of the Jews, and the king of Assyria repopulated the land by moving in people from other nations he had conquered. The Jews who were left in Israel intermarried with these foreign people and created a mixed race we know as Samaritans. They were actually considered unclean by the Jews, meaning that if you were touched by one of them you would be considered unclean as well.

With that said, let's scoot back to our parable.

＊*Who is asking Jesus a question?*

＊*What is the question?*

＊*What was his motivation in asking?*

At this time period, a lawyer was someone who was considered an expert in Mosaic law (which just means the Law of Moses in case that word looks unfamiliar). We don't necessarily know if he was being sarcastic or asking an earnest question, but he is definitely investigating in order to see what Jesus would say.

And here we see Jesus in His element. He is the last witness an opposing lawyer would want to have on the stand.

Jesus loves an open-ended question instead of a direct answer. Again, He knows the most powerful way to teach someone is to make a connection before giving a command. Jesus is speaking to someone who is obviously well-versed in the law, so He asks the lawyer to recite a passage of Scripture. Easy enough, right?

Jesus acknowledges the law, but then He goes a step further. He asks the lawyer to tell Him how he interprets the law. *What do you think it's saying? I know you can quote it, but what do you think it means?*

The lawyer, also in his element, gives a full-credit answer to Jesus. I bet he was feeling pretty smug, until Jesus basically said, "Yep! You've got it! That's all you need to do. Next?"

The lawyer is not ready to give up, so he asks Jesus a follow-up question. "Who is my neighbor, though? Huh? HUHHHH???" At this point, I imagine him turning toward the crowd and starting to hype them up to get them to cheer for him.

Note that one of those commands has to do with the way we treat other people. In other words, who exactly am I supposed to be nice to? Who should I love? Do I have to be nice to my enemies? Or are we legitimately talking about the people who just moved in next to me?

Jesus interrupts the party with a sweet story about a man who was beat up and left for dead on the side of the road. It's really the only option, as you know.

* *Where was the man going before he was robbed and attacked?*

* *Who is the first person to come across the man?*

\*What does he do?

**Priests** were direct descendants of Aaron in the tribe of Levi who performed numerous roles in the temple, the most important being sacrifices. **Levites** were members of the tribe of Levi not related to Aaron who assisted the priests.[10]

Niiiiiicceeeeee.

How about the next guy—what do we know about him? NOW WAIT. Don't answer yet. You will write *Levite* because that's what it says right there in front of you, but we are never satisfied with the surface level answer, are we? ARE WE? (Jesus taught me that trick.)

\*Think back to the twelve tribes of Israel. Do you remember that there was one brother who didn't get land? What was his name and why didn't he get the land?

See? Isn't it fun to do research? Then you get to discover that not one, but TWO "holy guys," one a priest, the other a Levite—people you'd think would care for the down-and-out—walked on the other side of the road from the almost-dead (and naked) man.

The irony is obviously not lost on the listener. Jesus is using two people who would be considered the heroes of society, and He is depicting them as the villains. And to make matters worse, He's about to make their enemy the hero.

\*What emotion does the Samaritan express when he comes across the man?

But that, in and of itself, is not what was required by the law. Jesus is going to show the real truth of the law. The point being made here is that not only did two people ignore a man in need, but the one who felt empathy followed through with action. He went to him. He bound him up and set him on his own animal. He paid for someone to take care of him. In fact, the money he gave the innkeeper was enough to take care of the man for two to three weeks. This was a sacrificial act bestowed upon a man who likely wouldn't have done the same for him.

It makes no difference what you know or believe—if you don't follow through with action, you have done nothing but take good notes for an upcoming exam. Even if you can describe every stroke to use in the pool in detail, that knowledge is useless unless you've actually been in the water.

You may be a lawyer who has all the facts, just as many Pharisees did. But will you truly love your enemies? If you do, you will not pass them by. You will love them as yourself and as your neighbor.

*How does the lawyer respond to Jesus' question?*

When Jesus asks him which person was the man's neighbor, the lawyer knew the answer. It was the one who stopped and took care of him. The one who loved him, showed empathy, and rescued him.

The lawyer couldn't even bring himself to say *Samaritan*.

Knowledge is useless unless it is put into action.

The injured man might have chosen to be left on the side of the road rather than be touched by a man who would make him unclean. The innkeeper could have refused to speak to the Samaritan or take his money. He didn't have to trust that the Samaritan would come back with the rest of the money.

*What, specifically, did the priest and the Levite do when they came across the injured man?*

Jews in this time are very familiar with the fact that Samaritans are not their neighbors. They make a point of walking extra miles to avoid Samaria when they travel.

Ironically, in this parable, they did the same to one of their own.

Jesus is making a blunt and undeniable point: your neighbors are the people in front of you who have a need, regardless of who they are.

But again, those words are spoken to people who may or may not have understood how to connect them to their lives.

Fortunately, Jesus is about to rock the boat (literally, but you'll have to wait a few days for that one) by showing them exactly how mercy walks. And trust me, there's no getting around it this time.

DAY 5
# HIS LOVE FOR EVERYONE

Get through today, and you'll get a whole two days off. (Unless you're doing this an hour before your group meets. You're welcome here too.)

\* *Find Luke 7 and read verses 1-10. Who is sick?*

\* *As a reminder, what is a centurion?*

\* *When the centurion heard about Jesus, who did he send to find Him and beg for healing?*

\* *What reasons did the men give to prove that the centurion was worthy of a miracle (v. 5)?*

\* *What happened when Jesus got close to his house (vv. 6-8)?*

### CENTURION

An officer in the Roman army who was usually in charge of one hundred soldiers. In the New Testament world, centurions were often seen positively.[11]

Although he is a Roman soldier, the centurion obviously cares about the Jewish people and has earned their trust and respect by honoring their faith. Maybe you've read these passages before, but hopefully you have a better backdrop now that we've been studying the culture of Jesus' day, and you have a greater depth of knowledge for why this is such a significant event.

A few years ago, my family was at the beach, and it was absolutely packed with people from every race, nationality, family size, and so forth. I imagine that our faiths varied dramatically as well. We all acknowledged each other and gave appropriate greeting smiles without having any emotional investment in one another.

All of a sudden, there was complete chaos. People were screaming and pointing at the water. It didn't take long to realize that there was a man on a surfboard who was a good bit away from the shore. Evidently he had missed the lifeguard's warning issued a few minutes prior.

As a result, he was now unknowingly floating around without realizing there was a shark riding shotgun beside him. Like, RIGHT beside him.

I'm not kidding when I tell you that at least one hundred people instinctively ran to the shore. Some walked a few feet into the water. Some screamed and waved and tried to get his attention. And some people stood back and filmed. I was a solid combination of the latter two options.

Within a matter of minutes, the man looked up and realized that either the entire beach was marveling at his surfing ability or trying to tell him he was being circled by an actual (not small) shark.

I looked around as people fell into different roles, shouting out jobs to one another as if they had been a team for years. No one yelled, "I don't want to be on waving duty!" Because at that point, there were two options: either they worked together, or this was going to end with national television coverage. And just like that, they formed a system which successfully alerted the man and then continued to motion for him to turn certain ways depending on where Jaws was.

When he was a few feet away from shore, everyone started clapping, and his family ran to hug him. I cried. A lot of people did, so don't make fun of me. It's the same reason I get choked up when ambulances or funeral processions pass by and strangers pull off to the side of the road.

We have a common goal that surpasses any of our differences.

And then we go back to our towels and our lanes and easily forget the line between crisis and conversation.

The point is there was something that needed to be done, not just talked about.

I love the way Jesus taught those around Him by using specific people to publicly announce a concept that would be entirely counter to their beliefs. And guess what? The people Jesus cared for weren't the kids who were typically moved to the front of the class.

He wanted people to see true faith in action—to have real-life examples of what it looked like. And He chose the sick, the sinners, the so-called enemy, and many other people who didn't "deserve" healing or favor.

*One of my favorite stories in Scripture happens in the Book of Luke. Find chapter 7, verse 36. Read through verse 50.*

She "was a sinner."

That's the introduction we get to a woman who has always been famous for her interaction with Jesus.

*Who asked Jesus to have dinner with him?*

There is no hesitation on Jesus' part; He comes to the house and reclines at the table with Simon the Pharisee.

As they're eating, an unexpected guest shows up (v. 37). It was likely that she was a prostitute, although the text never explicitly says that.

Before we get any further, let's clear up a few misconceptions.

Have you heard of Mary Magdalene? OK, she's the prostitute, right? The sinner? And now she's with Jesus and Simon?

Nope. Although some people believe this woman was Mary Magdalene, the text never specifies that. Furthermore, Mary Magdalene wasn't a prostitute. She was a woman who was possessed by demons and healed by Jesus (Luke 8:2). Also, her name isn't "Mary Magdalene;" it's just the way she is referred to in Scripture because her name is Mary and she is from Magdala. This is helpful because there are approximately 452 Marys in the Bible.

One last fun fact about Mary Magdalene: her name is mentioned twelve times in the canonical Gospels, which makes her one of the women mentioned most often. She was a loyal follower of Christ.

But back to the Pharisee's house. This is not Mary Magdalene. All we know at this point is that there is a woman at Simon's house who is likely a prostitute. She walks in and goes straight to the feet of Jesus. Again, let's just get a quick visual. She is not in front of Him while everyone stares at her in the middle of the room. She's behind Jesus, at His feet as He reclines.

By "reclines," I mean they all used to lay on their sides, leaning on their forearms when they were around the table.

*What did she bring with her (v. 37)?*

This is not a cheap perfume; she would have had to save up for it. I can't help but wonder if it was something she used in her professional life and if that's part of what she is offering to Him as a sign of her repentance and faith.

In verse 38, we see her crying so hard that her tears are getting all over His feet, so she starts to wipe them dry with her hair. She was a desperate, bold, humble woman who knew He was worth worshiping. She is kissing His feet (if we weren't talking about Jesus, I'd throw a red flag down right here because no) and anointing them with her perfumed oil. Y'all, there are SO MANY things that should not be happening here. She shouldn't even have her hair down.

At this point Simon is certain that Jesus isn't the Christ, let alone a prophet.

*Read Luke 7:41-43 and summarize the parable.*

It was a kind gesture to treat an honored guest by giving them a kiss of greeting, to anoint their heads with oil, and to have a servant clean their dirty feet, none of which Simon had done. But this woman, a sinner, was kissing His feet, anointing them with oil, and washing them with her tears.

*In general, what do you think Jesus is trying to translate to Simon with this story?*

*You, Simon ... the one who wants to do, do, do ... you failed to follow your own customs.*

She, on the other hand, actually did what Simon was supposed to, but she didn't do it because it was written down in a book of rules or expected. She did it because she knew she was a sinner, and she couldn't stop herself from worshiping the Messiah who could forgive her.

Do you see the difference? Remember, nothing Jesus ever teaches is surface deep.

In the Mosaic law (the old covenant), your motivation came second to your obedience. You simply obey.

In the new covenant, you obey out of the joy that comes from relationship with God. You obey not because it's required, but because it's impossible to refuse.

In other words: The old covenant demands obedience in order to be accepted by God. The new covenant says that once we accept Jesus and believe on Him, we will desire to be obedient to Him.

\* *What was her identity in verse 37?*

\* *Do you think she would have identified herself that way?*

\* *What do you think she wanted from Jesus? Take your best guess.*

\* *What did Jesus ask Simon in verse 44?*

I can't help it; those words get me every time: *Do you see this woman?*

When Jesus allowed her to anoint Him, Simon doubted because he knew that the true Messiah would *see* what she was.

In response, the Messiah praises her faith and asks the Pharisee if *he saw* who she was.

I have a feeling it was one of the first times she walked out of a room believing that she was worthwhile.

*Blessed are those who mourn.*

*Blessed are the meek.*

*Blessed are the merciful.*

*Blessed are the pure in heart.*

And, remember, blessed are those who actually listen to the lifeguard's announcements.

five

WEEK 5
# POWER: THE MIRACLE WORKER

It started the day my dad convinced me he had removed my left ear and was holding it in his fist.

I grabbed my head and screamed while he tried to explain that it was a joke. No. Jokes are funny. Pretending to remove an appendage doesn't fall in the joke category. He felt awful and apologized about twenty-five times before I went to bed.

Did I prank my kids with the same trick? Yes. Yes, I did. One of my girls cried, and the other one stared at my hand and said, "That's your thumb. Not an ear."

Seventeen years later, you could spend five minutes with them and point to the one who screamed and the one who looked bored.

The point is that nowhere in the "How to Be a Human" manual does it say it's physically possible for a body part to be pulled off and then put back on. It defies natural laws.

We would all say it isn't commonplace for a corpse to pop out of a casket during the funeral. I will say I read a story about a man who thought it would be hilarious to prank his family by making a recording to be shared during the actual burial. All of a sudden they hear his voice saying, "Hey, let me out of here! It's dark! Is that the priest talking? Let me out!"

Full credit awarded. That's pretty funny.

With that said, we don't wake up and imagine a situation where the laws of nature could be suspended or superseded. There aren't that many things in our lives that we assume won't change, and this is one of them.

I suppose that's why miracles are so impressive; they defy the very things we're certain will never change.

Anything outside of these laws is hard to comprehend as truth, which is why we call it a miracle.

We're going to be covering a lot of different miracles this week. And they're going to be all over the place—from healing obscure, unlikely people to shutting down storms. Jesus even resurrected the dead. Although the events were amazing, the goal of each of them was to show us His character and power.

What we don't want to miss is the message under the miracle; that's the part we can apply to our lives.

Stay tuned.

# GROUP SESSION GUIDE

## SESSION 5: REVIEW WEEK 4 HOMEWORK

* What new things did you grasp from the Scripture this week in your homework?

* Day 1: Name three of the reasons that Jesus came to earth.

* When you think about God's grace and how He knows we aren't perfect, do you feel relief? Anxiety? Unpack it a bit.

* Day 2: Which of the "Blessed are …" in the beatitudes stands out to you the most? Why?

* When we talk about Jesus tightening the reins on the law, what do we mean?

* Day 3: Which of the more "colorful" laws that we described was your favorite? The approved distance to move your ladder on the Sabbath? The mirror prohibition?

* How does our society, like the culture in Jesus' day, often place greater emphasis on the outside rather than the inside?

* Day 4: Did you learn anything new in our discussion of the parable of the good Samaritan? Tell your group about it.

✳ Day 5: How did Jesus react to the self-righteousness of Simon the Pharisee? If you had to insert yourself in this story and play the part of one of the characters, are you more likely to identify with the woman or with Simon? (If you said you identify with Jesus, we've got some other things to iron out.) Tell us why.

**WATCH SESSION 5 (VIDEO RUN TIME 17:01)**

## DISCUSS

✳ What part of the video spoke to you the most? Why?

✳ In times of healing, it can be easy to focus on the miracle—the restored sight, the extreme conversion. But ultimately the focus is on Jesus. How do you keep your eyes on Him? Do you have a daily rhythm that helps you focus your thoughts on God?

✳ Angie says, "God's got better things for us than we can imagine for ourselves." In times of pain, it can be hard to keep this truth in mind. What would it look like for you to apply this truth to a hard place in your current situation?

✳ Thinking of the Mark 2 story of the paralytic, tell your group about a time when you were metaphorically carried to Jesus by your community or a time when you metaphorically carried a friend to Jesus.

Video sessions available for purchase or rent
at LifeWay.com/Matchless

DAY 1

# THE "SMALL" MIRACLES

Jesus performs a lot of miracles in His time on earth. Although we have written testimony of a few dozen, there's reason to believe that number is actually higher.

> *When you think about Jesus performing miracles, what's the first one that comes to mind?*

> *Is that something you have ever prayed would happen in your life?*

> *When you have asked God to perform miracles, what were they related to?*

Several different words are used in the Bible to describe miraculous events: *sign, wonder, work, mighty work,* and *power*.[1]

I may be completely wrong, but I'm going to take a guess. You put something really huge (walking on water, calming a storm, or feeding five thousand people) for the first one, but your third question revolved around a physical healing for yourself or someone else.

I see myself in a sterile room no bigger than 6'x5,' and I'm listening to a woman with a stethoscope tell my sister that she is cancer-free.

In that miraculous moment, only three women were present. There were no crowds, no fanfare, no water turning to wine. What brings me to my knees isn't that He could be big; it's the inexplicable reality that He makes Himself small enough to fit into hospital rooms. How could such a great God be present in such a personal, quiet way?

Don't get me wrong—these are all true and powerful miracles, but for some reason the "big" ones aren't as emotional or shocking to me. That sounds strange to say, I guess, but in some way, those feel logical and appropriate to me; a big God performs dramatic and seemingly impossible things. In some sense I can get my head around an all-powerful God displaying His divinity this way—what seems impossible to me is that He did the small things.

> *Have you ever had anything happen in your life that you would define as a miracle? What was it?*

Every miracle Jesus performs is for a specific purpose, and He never displays His power for power's sake alone.

But how do His miracles relate to our lives now, and what keeps us from praying for and believing that they are still possible?

Well, for one thing, He isn't standing next to us. Noted as a disadvantage.

Do you remember Isaiah? Let's go visit him again. The man has definitely been given a huge role in prophesying about the coming Christ—just wait until we get a little further.

*For now, read what he says in 35:5-6 and write down the four miraculous things Isaiah says the true Messiah will perform.*

1.

2.

3.

4.

Remember, Jesus is deliberately and perfectly fulfilling the Old Testament promises of a Savior, but they probably aren't ones that the Jews would have been particularly concerned with—unless they were indications that the Messiah was capable of being a domineering King who would rescue them from oppression.

Keep that in mind as we talk through one of my favorite miracles in Scripture.

---

**SOME INTERESTING TIDBITS THAT YOU MAY OR MAY NOT ALREADY KNOW:**

1. Most miracles Jesus performed happened instantaneously.

2. He was never unsuccessful when He performed a miracle.

3. He never denied healing to someone who asked for it.

4. He healed people who didn't ask for healing.

5. He healed people He wasn't physically near.

6. He healed people who doubted He could.

7. He healed people who would've been considered His enemies.

8. He often performed miracles when He was just "passing by."

9. He performed miracles after being interrupted by people along the way.

10. In healing people, He bucked the system, but it wasn't just to rebel. His motive was to show love and compassion.

*Turn to Mark 10:46-52 and read through it. Write a summary of what happened.

*Now, write down ANYTHING that stands out to you. It could be the fact that he has an odd name. Take a couple minutes and pray as you read, asking the Lord to speak to you through His Word.

I love it. You're getting bolder about allowing yourself to dig into the Word, aren't you?

*Write verse 47 below:

*What does Bartimaeus call Him?

Are you ready for this? This is the only place in Mark where anyone calls Jesus by the title, "Son of David," and everyone who heard that term knew exactly what He meant—that phrase was reserved for the coming Messiah.[2]

*Bartimaeus, the blind man, saw Jesus as the Son of God.*

He saw more than the Pharisees.

I imagine the scene to look like it would if a modern-day celebrity was trying to go somewhere with a couple bouncers surrounding Him. They kept an eye on the crowd, making sure Jesus didn't waste His time with the poor and sick. I can't think of many times a celebrity would stop dead in his tracks and turn his attention to one unlikely person, holding up his entourage to speak to a random fan. It wasn't a quiet moment—I'm sure people clamored for Him no matter where He was. But Jesus heard the voice of one man who had the courage to believe.

*"Have mercy on me!"* He screams.

They try to silence him, but he only screams louder. This may be his only chance for healing, and he knows full well that the Healer is near.

*"Have mercy one me!"* His desperation fills the air.

And Jesus stops.

He tells His disciples to allow the man to come to Him, and they call him over.

Why wouldn't Jesus just walk over to him? I mean, the poor guy is blind, and He's the God of the Universe. He could have just hovered and floated over to him. I mean, there were options.

But He doesn't. He stands still.

Bartimaeus immediately throws off his cloak and runs toward the sound of Jesus' voice—the cloak that was one of his only possessions. The cloak that warmed him at night and spread out for coins during the day.

The cloak that reminded him everyday that he was dependent on man to have mercy on him. The cloak of his old life—the life of an outcast and a sinner.

The cloak that he would never need to wear again; the mercy of God would cover him now.

He was no longer a beggar; he was one of God's children.

But he had to walk to Jesus in response to the invitation. Out of faith, he left what he had clung to and clung to what he had now.

From blindness to sight, darkness to light. The healing that came from the faith of a man that everyone had walked past for years.

There's no way to know if anyone else ever knew him as anything other than a beggar, but Jesus makes it clear that the man has value, worth, and identity. He calls him by name, as He does for us.

It is no small thing for God to call you by name.

And He does, beloved.

He is a great God who made Himself small enough to be personal.

Then the eyes of the blind shall be opened ...

*Son of David, have mercy on us all.*

DAY 2
# CHANGING WATER TO WINE

Sometime last year, Nashville made it legal to sell wine in grocery stores. If you live in a place that has allowed this forever and it seems like a small thing, let me assure you, it was a THING. A short time later, it was decided that alcohol (both in liquor stores and grocery stores) could be purchased on Sundays. This was hotly debated and led to dramatic back-and-forth about whether or not it should happen, but I will say it led to a hilarious photo that continues to bless me to this day.

Most of the grocery stores ended up moving their water section to a different area to make room for the wine, but in one store the aisle headings hadn't quite caught up yet. After the wall of wine was set up, the sign above still said "Water," which resulted in many people posting pictures on social media with phrases like, "Jesus has been here!"

Most of us know the old "water into wine" phrase, but like so many other snippets of stories or Bible verses that have worked their way into our culture, it's easy to miss the significance of Jesus' first miracle.

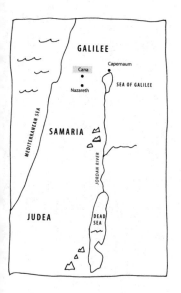

 * *Before we even talk about it, go ahead and write down anything you remember about the story. If you write absolutely nothing because you've never heard of it, that's OK too.*

 * *Flip on over to John 2 and read verses 1-11. Why is Jesus at the wedding?*

It's always this way with the Lord. He will never push His way into our lives; He must be invited. I love that Jesus performed His first miracle at a wedding. It's no coincidence that when He comes again, He'll come to claim His church—His bride.

Jesus was likely related to either the bride or the groom in some way, but we're never told the connection directly. It's important to know that in this time period, weddings went on for days, and it was shameful to run out of wine at any point during the celebration. (Unfortunately, that's exactly what happens here.) In fact, the guests could take legal action against the bride and groom if they weren't given the appropriate amount of vino.

Obviously, Mary is invested in the newlyweds and wants to spare them the embarrassment. She only says a few words to Jesus, and while I can't be one hundred percent certain of her intonation or intention, it seems to be a veiled request for Jesus to do something to fix it.

"They have no wine left."

I know these people. They insinuate a question but phrase it as a commentary.

"It sure is cold in here." "I wish I had a ride to the store." "This floor needs to be vacuumed."

In response, Jesus calls her "woman" and suggests that this matter has nothing to do with her or Him. Contrary to what you may imagine when you read this, the term He uses is actually very respectful and was commonly used when referring to women. However, it's not a term a son would use with a mother.

*What does she say in response?*

There is no sense of anger in her voice and no reason to believe this was a tense moment.

In fact, the significance of this statement is easy to miss: Jesus is telling her that their relationship was changing and that He will now defer only to His Father in heaven. He is gently explaining that her place in His life has shifted. Mary says nothing to Him in response. She speaks to the servants instead, and her comment is not without obvious deference: "Do whatever he tells you" (v. 5).

Also, I'm just going to say this on record: If I were God made flesh and living on the earth, I'd probably kick off my miracle ministry with something that packed more of a punch. Maybe becoming invisible or flying or setting stuff on fire.

But He didn't.

He chose a way that would symbolize the reason He was on earth.

*What is the traditional usage for the stone water jars (v. 6)?*

A *mikvah* is a pool of natural water in which Jews bathe to restore ritual purity.[3]

The Jewish people were obligated to purify themselves in several situations. For example, if a woman gave birth or had her period, she would be considered unclean and would have to bathe in a *mikvah* in order to be considered clean. Anyone who came to the temple would also have to be immersed in the water before going inside so that they would be ceremonially clean before entering such a holy place.

*In verse 7, we read the first sentence Jesus speaks in Scripture with regard to performing a miracle. Who does He speak to?*

Jesus said to the servants, "Fill the jars with water." And they filled them up to the brim.
JOHN 2:7

Only Jesus knew the truth of what would happen on the cross and how these jars were a symbol of the state of our hearts.

Pour as much water as you can into the jars, but it will never be enough. It will give you a sense of temporary mercy, but it will never give the everlasting fulfillment that Jesus does.

With this miracle, Jesus was subtly explaining His mission on earth.

These water jars were normally used for ceremonial cleansing, in line with the Mosaic law. What Jesus did at this wedding was to show that His blood was the new covenant wine. Jesus had come to provide complete cleansing through His blood. At this wedding, Jesus replaced the old covenant water with new covenant wine.[4] This foreshadowed how Jesus' sacrifice on the cross would soon replace the need for old covenant ceremonial cleansing.

Jesus' blood pays for our sins and allows us to know God. No amount of washing can do that.

### And he said to them, "Now draw some out …"
JOHN 2:8

Jesus never explains the miracle, nor does anyone at the wedding ever acknowledge the miracle. In fact, no one does.

We should know that Jesus would never do this (or anything) without a profound symbolism woven through the story.

I love this detail: think about who knows He has performed a miracle.

Who do you think would be the most prepared to take instructions from someone at this wedding? Probably the people who are there to take instructions. He chose the servants. Again, upside down. Often the least likely people are the most likely to obey Him.

And they do. They fill everything to the brim. They have absolutely no idea that this is going to be a miracle. They're just obeying.

"The guy says they need more water. I don't really think that makes sense, but let's do it anyway." It's the kind of obedience that flies in the face of what we think is needed.

He then tells them to take some out and bring it to the master of the party—he's in charge of keeping things going.

Matthew Henry points out that the servants haven't tasted it, and the master didn't see it poured. There's no room for sleight of hand here.[5]

The head of the party congratulates the groom and totally credits him with saving the best wine for last. I have no idea what he said, but it's clear that nobody at the wedding knew that 1) Christ was among them and 2) that they had been present for His first miracle. The one that would mark the pages of the Bible and point to His deity. They were clueless.

As the party roared on and the guests credited the hosts for the best wine being saved for last, there were only a few people who knew what had happened.

The people sitting around the bride and groom came by way of invitation. They were chosen by the folks who were having the wedding.

But there, in the place of service, out of sight from the rest of the party, were the ones who didn't get an invitation to be guests. They were hired to work.

They weren't invited to be served—they were serving the invited.

Think about the way they were seeing the wedding as compared to the way the guests were. Do you think they were talking about the amazing food and the way the bride looked? Were they kicking back and enjoying the festivities? Nope. They were making sure that the glasses stayed full and that everyone's needs were met.

They didn't come expecting to receive.

They didn't come expecting greatness.

I imagine Greatness came looking for them for exactly that reason.

## DAY 3
# CALMING THE STORM

Another day, another miracle. Love it.

One of my favorite quotes is by Albert Einstein, and it says, "There are only two ways to live your life. One is as though nothing is a miracle. The other is as though everything is a miracle."[6] I feel like he must've been a smart guy if he came up with that.

The story we're going to immerse (that was an intended pun that will make sense later) ourselves in today is actually one of my favorites for a lot of reasons. There's just so much going on and so many pieces to pull apart. We've seen Jesus make a party a whole lot more fun, and now we're going to see Him sleep. I'm here to provide you with endless amounts of "exciting Jesus" stories. But honestly, the seeming ordinariness of some of these stories can be one of the best parts—even though they're all amazing, they aren't so disconnected from our lives that we can't make sense of them.

Fun fact about me: I'm terrified of flying. When people ask me why that's the case, I feel like it's my opportunity to make a PSA explaining that we're trapped in a metal bus that's trying to defy the way ACTUAL GRAVITY works. In what scenario is unpredictably bouncing around on clouds at a cruising level of thirty thousand feet not scary? Also I'm very familiar with the "ding" system. One ding means we can go to the bathroom. A high ding means we've reached our cruising level. Three low dings mean we're going down, and it's every man for himself.

In all seriousness, it's not uncommon for me to have major panic attacks on really turbulent flights. I have to sit by the window to keep the plane up (by making sure I can see the ground). And as long as it's a nice day and smooth, I'm totally fine. It's just when it's stormy or super bumpy that makes me panic. Let me be clear: I've grabbed the person next to me and alternated between trying to breathe and screaming while tears fall on both of us. Let's just say that on more than one occasion a flight attendant has offered me a free gift from the vine.

It's genuine terror. The worst I ever feel in my life. It's just so out of my control and evidently out of the pilot's as well. Nature is unpredictable and certainly a force that we know we can't overcome.

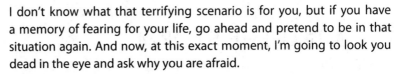

I don't know what that terrifying scenario is for you, but if you have a memory of fearing for your life, go ahead and pretend to be in that situation again. And now, at this exact moment, I'm going to look you dead in the eye and ask why you are afraid.

You would probably do exactly what I would in turbulence: stare at the person as if his/her head had just caught on fire.

As the plane drops twenty thousand feet over and over, everyone realizes that this has gone wrong, and it's not going to end well. They're staring at each other and acknowledging the fact that they will never see their loved ones again. They're hysterical. And then an announcement comes over the loudspeaker: "We have just gotten word that the pilot has been asleep for the last hour. We have woken him up, but he is confused about all of the mayhem that happened while he was napping. He has found the correct altitude, so things will be smooth now. Thank you for flying Galilee Air, and have a pleasant rest of the day" (4 dings).

 ＊ *Let's bring that incredulity to Mark 4:35-41. Read and summarize the story.*

 ＊ *What question does Jesus ask the disciples?*

JESUS IS ASLEEP. ON A COMFORTABLE CUSHION.

When they wake Him up, He finds them all so worked up about the whole near-drowning thing. I think we can agree that the question Jesus asks them is strange, but it's one He still asks us every day. *Why didn't you think I would rescue you? Did you think I didn't care?*

 ＊ *What are some situations in your life where you were desperate for help and convinced that Jesus was asleep?*

I've had moments of sheer panic when it didn't seem like He was going to come through. In those moments, I'm not sure Jesus' response to the disciples would have felt comforting to me: *Why are you so afraid? Do you really still not have faith in me?*

Spoiler alert: Jesus knew why they were afraid.

He was inviting them into a deeper conversation about trusting Him while also recognizing that they haven't stopped believing in Him. They have faith; it's just small. He's asking them to ask themselves that question: *why am I afraid?*

Here are a few things that make the story a lot more interesting.

\* *What does Jesus say to them in verse 35?*

He basically says, *Let's go. Get in the boat, because we're headed somewhere. We have a destination, and I'm telling you that we're going to end up there, so climb on in.* It isn't a maybe situation; it's Jesus essentially saying there is no other option but to arrive on "the other side" (v. 35) safely.

I know Jesus doesn't give those guarantees to us in the same way, but ultimately that's because we have different definitions of "the other side" (v. 35).

Sometimes that destination doesn't feel as reassuring as it should, does it? I wish I could say it always did, but the truth is I suffer from anxiety and depression, and they fight hard to keep hope at a distance.

You know I like to talk about reading the Bible as someone who is curious, right? Well I want to show you what I mean and see if it sparks anything new in the way you approach the Bible.

OK. Verse 35. Pretty straightforward. It was evening, and He told the disciples to get in the boat.

\* *Read through verse 36 a few times, and write down any words or phrases that make you wonder why they're there or what they mean.*

And if this activity feels weird, don't worry. It might just not be your style. Which means your style is wrong, but you don't have to leave the study because GRACE.

I'm curious what the phrase, "just as he was" means. Also I never pictured this story with other boats.

\* *Do the same thing you did for verse 36 with each of the remaining verses, and then we're going to wrap this baby up.*

*verse 37:*

*verse 38:*

*verse 39:*

*verse 40:*

*verse 41:*

I bet you found stuff. I wish I could compare answers with you. It's so interesting to see how Scripture speaks to people in different ways—even depending on where that person is at that particular place and time in life.

I wrote down several things, like "Where is the stern?" "Why did they call Him Teacher?" "What does the word *peace* mean in this verse?" "What was the tone of their voices? Angry? Desperate?"

Jesus asks them why they are afraid. First: He already knows the answer. Second: Of course they are. In Matthew, they wake Him and ask Him to save them (which seems to indicate that they believed He could), but in the other two accounts, their priority seems to have been somewhere else, and I wonder if you can relate.

　＊*What did the disciples ask Jesus as they woke Him up (v. 38)?*

*I believe You can save me, but I don't know if You even care.*

*Are You sleeping because You aren't afraid of the storm or because You don't care what happens to me?*

I think those are fair questions, ones we all have to wrestle with in our lives.

Just a few more things I want to note before we finish. Keep in mind that (as it is with every miracle) Jesus could've chosen to act in an infinite amount of ways.

　＊*Think about how this story is similar to the wedding at Cana based on the way it happened. Anything stand out?*

I noticed that Jesus chose to invite people into the miracle and then wait for them to come to Him. We aren't helpless bystanders without access to Jesus: "For we do not have a high priest who is unable to sympathize with our weaknesses, but one who in every respect has been tempted as we are, yet without sin" (Heb. 4:15). We serve a God who is not unfamiliar.

When Jesus rebukes the disciples, He isn't doing it to shame them. He is using the situation to teach and challenge people He loves and fights for.

Notice that Jesus uses the word "afraid" when speaking to the disciples. After He calms the storm, they have "great fear" (Mark 4:41). Their fear of Jesus at this moment, or in the Greek, *phobeo*, strikes a balance between being afraid or timid and awe or great reverence.[7]

You may think, *Well, of course they did. They just saw Him quiet a sea. I'd probably be afraid and in awe and convinced He could perform miracles and that would settle that. I mean, He's God, or He isn't, and that pretty much confirmed the answer. Who would doubt if they got to see it firsthand?*

*\* Head over to Matthew 8:1-4. Now read verses 14-17. Then look at verses 23-27, the parallel story Matthew penned.*

Y'all. If you've ever doubted that Jesus can perform miracles and you're hard on yourself because you don't think you have enough faith, I want you to remember those who walked alongside Jesus were afraid in spite of the fact that they had already witnessed MANY miracles in person.

But you and I both know it's different when you're the one in the boat, because it just may be that He doesn't care enough about you to intervene.

These are small words to describe a huge statement, but it's the only way I can think to say it: Since before the beginning of time, He has known more about you than you will ever know. As a believer in Christ, know that He loved you before you loved Him, and in every moment of your life, regardless of what it feels like, He is never far from you. You, my sister, are His beloved creation, and one day He's going to take you to the land He has promised you.

I know, because that's what the five dings mean.

I love you without knowing you, and I'm proud of your hard work. Can't wait to be with you again tomorrow!

DAY 4

# MIRACLES FOR TWO DAUGHTERS

Today is going to be a good one, y'all. God writes the best stories.

We're going to meet a couple of people whose lives intertwined in the most unexpected way possible. They couldn't have been more opposite; one is an outcast, and the other is a respected leader in the church. One is considered worthy, and the other isn't.

If we've learned anything about Jesus' world and the mantra of the old covenant, it's that what's happening on the outside is what really matters, right? It's what defines you, and it doesn't change. If you have leprosy, you're a leper. If you've committed adultery, you're an adulteress. What you do is who you are. Your value comes from your actions and status, not your intentions or motivation.

With that in mind, I can understand why people were a little resistant when a stranger pranced into town and spent the majority of His time with the sick and rejected. It's not the ideal branding strategy if your goal is to be powerful.

> *Open up your Bible to Matthew 7:1-5 and write a summary of what it says.*

Well that puts a kink in things, doesn't it? If we judge others, then we'll be judged to the same degree? I need to realize I've got something about myself that could be worse? Inconceivable (pronounced with "th" instead of "c" for those of you who will appreciate the reference*).

*For you *Princess Bride* aficionados.

> *Find Mark 5 and read verses 21-24. (This passage may sound familiar to you. We talked about it in our Session 3 teaching video, so you've got a leg up on our work here.)*

> *What do we learn about him before we're given his name?*

> *In verse 22-23, there's a guy waiting for Jesus to arrive. What is his name, and what does he want Jesus to do for him?*

We know there's a crowd waiting for Jesus. I've read this story many times, and for some reason, I've always pictured Him with a bunch of rabbis and scribes gathering around the shore with Jairus, shouting out to Jesus and begging Him to heal the little girl who was deathly ill. As I read it again recently, I realized Scripture never explicitly says that was the case. Maybe it was a group of "ordinary" folks who came to see what Jesus was all about. But it was clear that the "important people" were toward the front. I'm sure the ordinary people had prayer requests. I'm sure they each wanted some one-on-one time with Him, but it doesn't appear that anyone dared to push forward except for Jairus.

Obviously, Jairus had a dire need, but that doesn't mean he was the only one who did. (Maybe his status or fancy clothes made it seem like he "deserves" it more.) He falls at the feet of Jesus and makes it clear that he believes the Lord can heal his daughter. However, Jairus does have what could be a little bit of superstition or confusion about the way in which Jesus can heal.

> *What does Jairus specifically assume Jesus would have to do in order to make his daughter well?*

Jesus begins to walk with Jairus to the place where his daughter is fighting for her life, and everyone follows along—I'm guessing because they want to see if He can actually do it.

> *It isn't the trip any of them are expecting it to be. Read verses 25-29. What was the woman's issue?*

> *How long had it been going on?*

> *What did she do in an effort to be healed?*

> *What happened as a result?*

Let's sit there for a second. I want to make sure you have an accurate depiction of this woman and are thinking through the assumptions we can make about her life based on her physical situation. Because she was considered unclean (and obviously had been for many years), she

Jairus was a synagogue leader or ruler of the synagogue, meaning he was responsible for leading worship and giving instruction.[8]

Leviticus 15:25-30 explains why she was considered unclean.

probably would've been divorced from her husband (or had to refrain from marrying) and forced live outside the community. She wasn't permitted to have any contact with her old friends, nor was she allowed to go to the synagogue because anyone she touched would also become unclean.

I think she ran up from behind Jesus because she was ashamed of who she was, and she didn't want anyone to notice her. This was a huge risk. By law, she wasn't even supposed to be there, let alone in a crowd of people she could affect.

She's probably grateful that she is healed instantly because it means she can sneak away without being noticed. I'm sure she was desperate, but I also wonder if she believed Jesus wouldn't heal her if she asked because she was such "damaged goods." Furthermore, it's obvious that she has caught up with the crowd as they were rushing to save someone more "important" and "deserving."

*What happens in verses 30-32?*

He asks, "Who touched me?" (v. 31). The disciples remind Him that there's a massive crowd of people around Him and urge Him to keep moving.

And no, He doesn't need her to identify herself because He's curious. He knows exactly who she is.

*What does she do in verse 33?*

Here's the thing about healing: If you're going to tell people you've been healed, you have to be willing to tell them what you've been healed *of*.

Dozens of eyes are on her as she answers. I can't imagine what that must have felt like.

*Specifically what does it say she told Jesus?*

She didn't give a five second recap. She told the *whole* truth. We don't know what that included, but it was a confession—and not just for touching Jesus' hem.

*When she finished speaking, what did Jesus tell her to do?*

*What does He call her?*

This is the only time in Scripture that Jesus calls a woman by that name. And He is using it for one who was least likely to be considered His daughter—and least likely to believe she could be.

*What has made her well?*

*Take a guess at why Jesus might say that to her.*

I think there are a couple reasons: Jesus didn't want her to think it had been her hand on His garment that healed her. She didn't "sneak" a blessing. It was her faith that made her well—body and soul.

Garments, whether the robes of a Pharisee or the edge of His cloak, are external decorations, not internal belief.

I believe Jesus also wanted to make sure that everyone knew she was both healed and His.

Can't you picture this scene? Surely everyone there wasn't only amazed by the miracle; they were amazed at who had been chosen to receive it. And all the while, an innocent girl was about to die.

She did, in fact, die.

But Jesus knew He wasn't bound by time or space and that He had dominion over sickness and death.

The crowd had to acknowledge that this series of events didn't follow the typical patterns of rank. And with that, maybe they were even on their way to acknowledging that those patterns no longer existed.

No one there was more holy, more sinless, or less worthy of the love of Christ.

One was an innocent twelve-year-old girl, the daughter of a respected man; the other was a woman who had been ostracized for twelve years.

Can you see how beautiful this story is? Jesus was on the way to heal a very powerful man's daughter, and He stopped to tell an anonymous woman that she was the daughter of a more important Man.

DAY 5
# RAISING LAZARUS

Have you heard of Mary and Martha? If not, let me introduce you. They are quite a pair, these two. Let's head over to their house, because I have a feeling there's some good cooking going on.

*Go to Luke 10:38 and read through verse 42.*

Let me tell you the part that makes me laugh: Martha literally tattled on her sister TO THE SON OF GOD. Also, the Greek words used when she asks, "Don't you care?" are the same as the phrase used by the disciples in the boat. I think it's one of my go-to phrases when I'm scared.

When Jesus responds to Martha, He isn't condemning or shaming her for working. He is gently telling her that she is so busy worrying about all the "important" things that she has missed the most important thing.

You may teach Sunday School every week and make casseroles for potlucks. You might lead a Bible study and volunteer at the homeless shelter. Don't get me wrong, those are amazing things that bless the Lord and His kingdom.

*What's your motive? Are you intentionally serving the Lord without putting smiley-faced stickers on your obedience chart?*

I know we hear this question enough to have a knee-jerk reaction and say no, but pause before you do that and really consider your true answer:

*Do you feel like you can earn acceptance from Jesus by doing things?*

I'm not telling you to quit doing amazing things, but here's the question that's posed underneath this encounter: Are you serving the world so much that you've forgotten to serve God?

I'll admit that my brain says I'm being lazy when I'm not busy working. It's hard for me to sit still and relax because there are dishes in the sink and I'm worried the neighbor-kid is drinking bleach.

What the Lord is telling us is to abide in Him. We're to be so aware of His will and presence that our actions are a natural response. Mary was compelled to do that because she knew nothing around her mattered as much as sitting at Jesus' feet and listening to His voice.

That's hard to do when pots and pans are clanging and the casserole is burning.

It's all right, Janet. You can set down the spatula and know that you are loved by Jesus anyway.

Abide.

It's harder than it sounds, isn't it?

Mary and Martha aren't just people Jesus met once; they are actually some of His dearest friends. He stays at their house in some of the hardest days of His life. They have a brother named Lazarus; who, in my book, wins the award for best participant in a miracle.

The thing I want to bring up before we read Lazarus' story is that Jesus had genuine, human feelings. He laughed the way we do. He got angry the way we do. He came to be with us in the truest sense of the word.

There's no telling how many times Jesus, Lazarus, Martha, and Mary ate around a table together. Someone prepared a place for Him to sleep and said goodnight to Him. I daresay we can guess who did what in that scenario. He loved them in a deep, connected way.

*Read John 11:1-16.*

So, remember, the Pharisees are up in arms because Jesus has been performing miracles on the Sabbath and telling people He's the Son of God—all things that apparently didn't go over too well with these guys.

They wanted to kill Jesus and that isn't an ideal situation.

Jesus is heading toward what He knows will eventually be His death. This is the last time His feet will walk these roads before He goes to the cross. His disciples warn Him, telling Him it's too dangerous.

Mary, Martha, and Lazarus lived in Bethany, just a couple of miles from Jerusalem.

*When Jesus gets to Bethany, how long has Lazarus been in
his tomb (John 11:17)?

That number isn't random. Jesus knew what the rest of the Jews
believed: that after a person died, their spirit would hover around the
body for three days in the hope that the body would come back to life.

Three days.

He waited so that they would know for certain it was a miracle.

Martha runs to Him and mourns, saying that if He had been there,
her brother wouldn't be dead. He tries to explain that Lazarus will be
resurrected, but Martha doesn't understand that He means it literally.
He asks her if she believes He is the Son of God, and she tells Him she
does and then runs to find her sister.

*Mary then goes to the place where Jesus is (He hasn't
entered the village yet), and what does she do (John 11:32)?

Jesus sees the way the people are mourning, and when they bring Him
to the tomb of Lazarus, Scripture says He wept.

He wasn't weeping for Lazarus; He was weeping for those who were
grieving. He was also grieving over the fact that they didn't believe Him.

And it may have been more than that—He is staring at a tomb with the
knowledge that His fate will not look much different.

We don't know all of the things going through His mind, but it is clear
that He aches for those He loves when they are suffering.

Friend: if you don't hear another thing I say to you today, hear this: Jesus
knows the end of the story, but He grieves with us in the meantime.

*What does she say when Jesus asks to move the stone
away from the cave where Lazarus is buried (John 11:39)?

Claaaaaaaassic Martha.

*After the stone is moved away, what does Jesus do (John 11:41-42)?*

He knows God is able to perform this miracle, and He knows He will be able to perform another one in a very short time. He wants the people to believe in God so they will believe in His own resurrection.

"Lazarus, come out." He says, and with that, Lazarus comes out, still wrapped in his burial cloths. Jesus tells them to unwrap him, and that's the end of it.

Six days before Passover began, Jesus went to Bethany to be with Mary and Martha again. Of course Martha is serving.

*What does Mary do instead (John 12:3)?*

The amount of oil she poured onto the feet of Jesus was approximately a year's wages. Judas (one of the disciples) makes a fuss about how that money should have been given to the poor. He doesn't care about the poor; he cares about money. So much so that he would do anything to have it.

He will betray Jesus, and he won't be the only one.

And as Passover nears, the Son of God prepares for the day He will die.

For the day He will stumble with a heavy wooden cross tearing into His back, the scent of Mary's praise still on His feet.

six

WEEK 6
# PASSION: THE SUFFERING SAVIOR

This is the hardest week I had to write, and I'll tell you this: I cried. A lot. These are all things I've known for awhile—Jesus suffered through the last week of His life and was crucified for us. I can't stop singing a song that was almost always part of mass at my dad's church, "He takes away the sins of the world …"

But I don't imagine the suffering of Jesus every time I sing those words, nor do I often do that when I sing any song. There are many that move me emotionally, and I'll find myself with my hands in the air and tears dripping down my face. But things have shifted since writing this Bible study, specifically this week. I had to dig into commentaries and studies and different translations of Scripture, and I found things I didn't expect to discover. In other words, I wasn't ready to know what I do on this side. I study the Bible, and I have for years, but that doesn't mean I fully comprehend everything. We've talked about this, but comprehension is not the same as experience.

*Y'all.*

I met Him here.

I met Him as He shared His last Passover with His closest friends, knowing that they were all going to abandon Him, some in worse ways than others.

I met Him on the stand as He was questioned and charged with crimes He hadn't committed.

I met Him as His legs fought for every step toward the place where He would ultimately prove to be the true Messiah.

I met Him as He spoke one word and closed His eyes.

I felt His pain differently, and I celebrated the other side of the cross in a way I'm not sure I have before.

And I know this for certain—He takes away the sins of the world.

Let's start the Passion Week exactly where He did: just outside Jerusalem. Jesus' disciples were beside Him as He lifted Himself onto the most humble of creatures: a donkey, of all things.

Trust me, it wasn't by chance.

Are you ready to walk with Him? I'm right here with you, friend. And everything you're about to read happened because of you. You're there in the story, and I hope and pray you'll see yourself and meet Him in a way you never have before.

## GROUP SESSION GUIDE

SESSION 6: REVIEW WEEK 5 HOMEWORK

* What new things did you grasp from the Scripture this week in your homework?

* Day 1: Even though you may believe Jesus performed miracles, do they ever seem far away and irrelevant to your life? Explain. How does that affect your faith in Christ to do powerful things in and through you?

* What do you think constitutes a miracle?

* Day 2: Of all the miracles Jesus could have done as His first one, why change water into wine? What's the purpose and significance of this miracle?

* Day 3: When have you felt like chaos ruled, everything was crashing in, and Jesus was asleep at the wheel? How did you make it through that time, and what did Jesus do to reassure you of His presence and power? Or do you feel like He didn't?

* How have you seen fear affect your relationship with Jesus?

* Day 4: After the woman with the issue of blood was healed, Jesus called her "Daughter" (Mark 5:34). It's the only time in the Bible He called a woman by that name. What was so significant about Him addressing her in this way?

#MatchlessBibleStudy

✳ Day 5: How did Martha and Mary struggle with Jesus' timing in bringing Lazarus back to life? When have you faced difficult situations where your need and Jesus' timing didn't seem to match up? At some point have you been able to look back and see the purpose in Jesus' delayed response? Explain.

**WATCH SESSION 6 (VIDEO RUN TIME: 6:22)**

## DISCUSS

✳ What part of the video spoke to you the most? Why?

✳ Why does our faith hinge on the truth of the cross and the resurrection?

✳ Even after the other disciples told Thomas that Jesus was alive, Thomas wanted physical proof before he believed. When it comes to faith, are you a little like Thomas or a lot like him? Why?

✳ What are some doubts about Jesus that you've dealt with? How has Jesus met you in those moments and answered your concerns?

Video sessions available for purchase or rent
at *LifeWay.com/Matchless*

DAY 1
# THE TRIUMPHAL ENTRY

The streets are overwhelmed by the amount of people who have traveled to Jerusalem for Passover. The smell of animals, the sounds of people screaming, the throngs of strangers pushing past each other as they travel to the temple to worship. Voices were worshiping, singing the Psalms, and they were anticipating the day when they will once again celebrate how God rescued them from slavery through the blood of the Passover lamb.

**Hardly anyone notices an inconspicuous Man approaching the city, surrounded by men who look like the thousands of others there. But Jesus knew that today as He walked into the city, He was walking to His death.**

*Find Mark 11 and read 1-7.*

*What did Jesus ask the disciples to do for Him?*

Kind of a weird request, isn't it? "I'll just hang out here, and you guys go find me a donkey. He's tied up exactly where I'm telling you and if people ask, just tell them I need it. There's no way this could go wrong. Oh, and tell them I'll bring it back. I just need to borrow him. It'll all make sense later."

*Read Zechariah 9:9 and see if that puts this event in context.*

So beautiful.

Typically a victorious king would come into town on a horse, leading a procession of really powerful people, including the army that had just defeated the enemy. Everyone would have praised him, shouting in celebration. He then would have made a sacrifice in a temple to acknowledge the gods and basked in all of the adoration.

Cue Jesus sitting on a donkey and walking into the city with a couple of average Joes. Um, pretty sure that's not the way it's supposed to go.

Except it was. It always was. They just can't see it.

I love the details of Scripture, and this story doesn't disappoint. You've practiced this already, so I hope that you've been working on taking time to ask questions of the text while you read it. Here we see Jesus requesting a specific type of donkey—one that is tied up around the corner and has never been ridden. Donkeys that have never been ridden don't just let a stranger climb on them and show obedience; they have to trust the person first. And if the donkey was tied up, it probably means it was young or a little wild.

The disciples put their coats on the animal's back and watch as Jesus climbs on. Do you think they're all upset because this is the beginning of the end? No. They don't have a clue. It's just your average "steal a donkey" Sunday for them.

*Read Mark 11:8-10. Describe what happened as Jesus entered Jerusalem.*




As Jesus enters the city, there is a great commotion, and suddenly masses of people are shouting. Some are calling Him the Messiah. Some are begging for Him to save them. Some are throwing palm branches and coats on the ground. Some are celebrating the fact that Jesus represents the coming kingdom of their father, David.

*Hosanna! Hosanna! Glory in the highest!*

Imagine it.

Jesus looks into their eyes. He acknowledges and accepts that they are calling Him the Promised One. He realizes He is looking into the faces that may scream "Crucify Him!" in a few short days.

The accounts of this incident vary from Gospel to Gospel (as other stories of Jesus typically do), but I think Mark's is the funniest.

*Read verse 11.

The man definitely likes some detail, huh? *He walked in and looked around a little and then headed out because it was late.* I point this out to remind you that these are four different people who are writing

**HOSANNA**

is a Hebrew or Aramaic term translated "Save now."[1]

Spreading branches and cloaks before Jesus was a recognition of royalty.[2]

down accounts of this event (in this case, it was likely Mark writing down Peter's account). In Peter's mind, that was part of the story as he remembered it. It adds credibility. There's no apparent reason this detail needs to be part of Scripture. But it's important because we get to see a situation through his eyes.

> *In Matthew's version (head to Matt. 21), what also happened while they were in the temple (vv. 12-17)?

> *What did Jesus say in verse 13?

> *Once you've read it, go ahead and find yourself some Isaiah 56 and look at verse 7.

I'm not sure if I've mentioned this, but Jesus came to fulfill all of the prophecies from the Old Testament. I did? Sorry—my bad.

Every time He uses a phrase like, "It is written …" He is reminding them of the Scriptures they have heard for their entire lives. He's not making it hard for them to see that. "Hey, folks? You've read this already. Ta-da! It's Me! This is the donkey I told you about!"

Crickets.

But He's not done yet.

> *Review verses 14-17. He amped it up a little, didn't He? Who is upset and why?

But have no fear, Jesus is here. Yes. Have you never read that? If you want to lay eyes on this prophecy, feel free to hop on over to Psalm 8:2. Also, I want to imagine that He sometimes got a little sarcastic with the leaders. *Aren't you supposed to be the expert here? Surely you remember that if you really are …*

> *Now let's go to Luke 19:28.

His version is similar: donkey, crowds of people, and so on. But there are a few details added that give us a better understanding of the events that are around the corner.

*Read verses 38-39 and write down what happened in verse 39.*

*Tell them to stop. How dare You allow these people to call You King?* For most of Jesus' time on earth, He has discouraged people from doing that. But what He is telling the crowds, the scribes, the leaders, the rabbis, the Pharisees, and everyone else is the tipping point. Accepting the worship reserved for the Messiah was blasphemy and justification for crucifixion.

*Luke's version—that's the one that gets me. Find Luke 19 and read verses 41-44.*

Jesus is weeping for His children, His beloved, His sheep who have wandered astray. He knows what fate befalls them, and He knows the way they will be persecuted, defeated, and hated.

He has come to give them peace, but He knows they won't all choose it.

He has come to rescue them from the oppression of sin, but He knows many will choose to walk back into it.

The Passover is coming in a few days, and the irony of the situation isn't lost: they are celebrating freedom without realizing they are choosing to be slaves again.

*The blood of the Lamb shed for you.* Every doorway marked and a sea split in half for their safety. He will never stop loving the ones who refused to love Him, and that's why He cries.

It's the fourth day before Passover, and the Jews are doing what they always do on this day.

They are choosing the unblemished lambs that will be sacrificed on their behalf without knowing that the Savior of the world was in their midst.

A few hours prior they had been offering Him palm branches and praise, never realizing that they were watching the one true Lamb as He moved closer to the day when He would be sacrificed on their behalf.

*Father, forgive them. They don't understand.*

**Scripture records Jesus weeping three times:**
1. At Lazarus' tomb, John 11:35
2. Over Jerusalem, Luke 19:41
3. Before His death, Hebrews 5:7

DAY 2
# THE LAST SUPPER

I know yesterday had a lot of emotional moments. I don't want to miss this opportunity to set the record straight, because I know that it has been pressing on you since you finished.

I don't know if the donkey was ever returned. It will forever be a mystery. He probably did his job and went off to live his best life as "Jesus' chosen donkey."

Now that we've gotten that out of the way, let's see what happens after the triumphal entry. I don't know if you picked up on this, but in case you didn't, that's why we call it Palm Sunday.

I'll start with a confession: before I started working on this study, I saw a lot of names in Scripture and skipped over them. I'm going to be straight up honest with you: I didn't really care who they were because they were sort of secondary characters in the movie, you know? Like, no one was in the theater by the time the credits got to them. They're farther down than the second grips. No longer. I now realize that they are high enough on the list to see them before you've got your purse on and are pretending you don't see your popcorn on the floor.

> *Go to Exodus 4:24-26. Does that make more sense now? No? Me either. Sounds intense, though.*

> *Let's actually flip ahead a few pages to Exodus 12:1-28.*

I know, I know. It's a lot of reading. But I believe in you. There are going to be some details you might not understand, but I want to make sure you've got a good grasp on the rest. Let's have a fill-in-the-blank party. (Hint: These verses are from the English Standard Version. Janet, I know you want to fill in *every* blank perfectly, and I love that about you. )

> *Let's start at 12:1 and get through it together. Remember at this point, the Israelites were slaves in Egypt and God had told Moses He was going to rescue them and bring them to the land He had promised to them. This should help you tie up some of the information from yesterday and will point us straight in the direction we need to go.*

*12:3*... on the _____ day of this month every man shall take a _____ ... *5*Your lamb shall be _____ _____ ... *6*and you shall keep it until the _____ day of this month, when the whole assembly of the _____ ___ _____ shall kill their lambs at _____. *7*Then they shall take some of the blood and put it on the two _____ and the lintel [top] of the _____ ... *13*The _____ shall be a _____ for you, on the houses where you are. And when I _____ the _____, I will _____ _____ _____ ... *14*This day shall [become] for you a _____ _____, and you shall _____ it as a _____ to the LORD ... *15*_____ days you shall eat _____ _____ ... *17*And you shall observe the _____ of _____ _____, for on this very day I brought your _____ out of the land of _____. Therefore you shall observe this day, throughout your generations, as a _____ _____.

\* And then Moses repeated to the Israelites what God had told him in verses 21-28.

*26*And when your children say to you, "What do you mean by this _____?" *27*you shall say, "It is the sacrifice of the _____ _____, for he _____ _____ the houses of the _____ ___ _____ in _____.

You are a champ. You are an Old Testament champ. And yes, Janet. I see your hand raised to tell me that you did it from memory.

When we left off, the religious leaders were plotting to kill Christ, and He was about to gather His disciples for the last supper.

Well, that's what we call it. I mean we all know the painting by Leonardo da Vinci, right? But it's not like the disciples were hustling and bustling to prepare things knowing it was the last supper they would ever have with Jesus. They were just preparing a Passover meal to celebrate the same way the thousands of people around them were celebrating.

If you look at what you just filled in, you'll notice a couple of days where certain things are to be done in remembrance of the Exodus.

**LEAVEN**

was a small piece of fermented dough that was used to ferment other dough to make it rise.[3]

For the first seven days, they are not to eat bread with leaven. Why? Why not? Leaven is awesome! Well, here's the reason: when the Jews were escaping from Egypt, they were kind of in a hurry because the Egyptians were trying to kill them and all, so they didn't have time to wait for their bread to rise … hence, the Festival of Unleavened Bread.

The first day of that celebration is Passover. (I realize you're far enough along to not need a definition here, and I AM BEAMING WITH PRIDE.)

*Read Matthew 26:17-18 really quick. Does it make more sense now?*

Are you starting to understand that this entire week is tied to the Exodus? Is that something you've known since Sunday School? Well, I didn't. And the thing about the Gospel writers not all being disciples still messes with me a little.

After they have prepared the meal, Jesus and His twelve disciples gathered around a nondescript table in the upper room of a house, not a palace. Jesus is keeping a low profile, not parading around. It is just as it was always going to be, with our Lord realizing the weight of what He was about to teach them, knowing that it would become a symbol of people's faith in Him, and it would help generations remember the significance of what was about to take place.

*Head to Luke 22:14-15. What does Jesus say as the supper begins?*

That's a new way to kick off a dinner, isn't it? Why didn't anyone ask why He's excited and what He's going to suffer?

*Jesus says that the cup that is poured out for you is the*

_____ _____.

Did you know that the word *testament* means "covenant"?[4] It's true. He is telling them that the wine is to be used in remembrance of the way His blood replaced the Old Testament with the New.

Does that change the way you'll take the Lord's Supper? It isn't just to remember Jesus. The Lord's Supper honors the fact that His blood and body were given to fulfill the promises of the Old Testament. It's to show us what the Law had meant all along. It was always about God's grace, mercy, and love instead of the infinite amount of rules that people had invented and enforced.

Go to 1 Corinthians 11:17-34 to read Paul's words about the importance of how we take the Lord's Supper.

*Turn to John 13:31-38. (Don't worry, we'll talk about verses 1-15 in just a second.)

Sweet Peter. He really just wants to understand. He can't imagine Jesus leaving, and he begs to go with Him.

*In response, what does the Lord say Peter will do?

*Read John 13:1-15. What does Jesus do at the last supper?

*You are going to understand this one day.*

*What will they understand (vv. 14-15)?

Jesus goes on to tell them that one of the men at the table, whose feet He had just washed, would betray Him.

No one knew that Satan had entered Judas, nor did they know why he left the table.

But Jesus did. And in a few hours they would too.

DAY 3
# THE GARDEN

Before the last supper ends, Jesus lifts His eyes to heaven and prays to His Father.

*Find John 17:1 and write down what it says.*

*Who is this prayer intended for? Who isn't it intended for (v. 9)?*

*Read verses 20-21. Who else does Jesus pray for? What does He ask? Why?*

Do you understand how radical this is?

Jesus isn't praying for His chosen people; He is beseeching God on behalf of those who believe in His name.

That's the requirement. Full stop.

Jesus doesn't claim Jewish people as His flock because they have gone astray. They don't recognize the voice of their Shepherd.

*Read Matthew 26:30-35.*

You may have recognized those four important words: "For it is written."

*What does verse 32 say as a follow-up to that statement?*

Jesus knows all that was about to happen, including that within a matter of hours, Peter will deny knowing Him three times. Jesus tells him so. Peter can't believe it's true, but when he hears the rooster crow he realizes what he's done.

*What does Jesus ask His disciples to do for Him
  in Matthew 26:36?*

*Who does Jesus take with Him as He goes to pray (v. 37)?
  What is His request to them (v. 38)?*

Jesus speaks to them in what was no doubt the most emotional plea of their time together: *My soul is sorrowful to the point of death. Stay with Me. Watch with Me.*

He wants them to be near Him, and He is comforted by the idea that He isn't alone as He prays. He takes only a few steps before falling to the ground, His face pressed into the dirt as He asks His Father to spare Him.

*If it is possible, let this cup pass from me.*

Three times Jesus walks away to pray, and every time Jesus comes back to check on His disciples, they are sleeping.

You guys, this isn't the best way to convince Him—let alone the rest of the world—that you care.

Here's the deal: Jesus has a terrible marketing strategy. Let me compare it to an infomercial because that's obviously the most logical approach.

Imagine this with me: I am intrigued by the vacuum being sold for four easy payments of $29.99. The models are smiling and pointing to features as the host excitedly explains that this is a breakthrough in technology and has done everything from disintegrating Cheerios® to saving marriages. And I am a believer within three minutes. This is exactly what I have been waiting for, and once I grab one of the 128 127 126 that are left, I know for sure that it'll be a turning point in my life.

I am about to commit when I hear the host ask the model how she has liked using the vacuum in the past few years. I stop entering my credit card information because I feel like her answer is going to convince me that I'll look like her within six-to-eight weeks or forty-eight hours if I have a registered warranty and choose expedited shipping for just two extra payments.

"This? I've actually never seen it before."

> "In the Old Testament, the cup is referred to symbolically as punishment and judgment (Isa. 51:17; Jer. 25:15-29; Rev. 14:10). In this case, it refers to Jesus' death on the cross."[5]

Huh? The host stares at her in shock. "Yes, you have. I've seen you use it. Why are you saying that?"

The model shakes her head, denies it again, and poses with one hand on her hip and the other on the adjustable handle. Her manicure is perfect, which, I assume, was done by the vacuum.

The host is now incredulous and irritated because the sales have come to a standstill. She tries one last time, but she gets the same answer.

The background music gets louder as the host awkwardly motions producers to help.

They send another model out but then they realize she had actually sold hers online for two dollars, which isn't helpful. She goes so far as to bring the competitor's vacuum out to knock down the featured item.

Twelve people are called to testify about the wonders of this product, and by the end, every one of them has walked off set before giving the pitch.

The takeaway is that the people who were supposed to know the product better than the people at home have gone rogue. The producer is tearing up scripts. The cameraman is faking malfunctions. The host is crying. The audience continues to *ooh* and *aah* because when they replaced actual people with a track, they did not consider all of the possible outcomes.

Y'all. Why would anyone want it?

Jesus is asking His followers to be with Him, for Him, and willing to walk wherever He does. And the results of those requests aren't what you would expect considering that He's the Son of God.

After His third prayer, Jesus comes back to the sleeping disciples and tells them to stand up. He has fully submitted to His Father's will, and the time is at hand.

> *Then he came to the disciples and said to them, "Are you still sleeping and resting? See, the time is near. The Son of Man is betrayed into the hands of sinners. Get up; let's go. See, my betrayer is near."*
> MATTHEW 26:45-46, CSB

This group of soldiers would have included Roman soldiers and temple police (John 18:3).

As Jesus is speaking, a crowd surrounds Him. There are priests and elders among the group of soldiers, all waiting for a sign from Judas in order to arrest the right Man.

Jesus and Judas. Between the two of them was only the night air and memories of the intimate moments that wouldn't make it into the red words in the Bible because they were personal. No one could understand what they had been through together.

I don't know who the slowest disciple was, but they did—and likely teased him about it.

I have no idea which disciple ate the most or made everyone laugh.

I don't know their inside jokes or secret handshakes.

I haven't a clue how many late-night conversations there were or how many times a day they had to stop because one of them had the smallest bladder, which had been a running joke for the last three years. I don't know if there was one guy who women always flirted with and, without exception, was teased by the rest of the crew as soon as they were alone.

It's easy to recite stories we've heard time and time again without giving them a chance to breathe. This isn't just about a God who came to die for us; it's about the Christ who came to live with us.

This wasn't a stranger walking up to Him. Jesus knew his face, his hands, the way he walked, and the fact that he was the hardest to wake up. He knew what he liked to eat and what he said at night just before he went to sleep.

They were a ragamuffin gang, that's for sure. But they knew they were special and probably walked around with their heads high and shoulders back. "Yeah. We're with the Guy you've heard of. He only picked twelve of us, and I'm one of them. I'll see what I can do to get you a backstage pass."

If we're to truly understand Christ's humanity, we have to acknowledge that it wasn't just Him and twelve other guys. For three years Jesus was, in His humanity, just one of the thirteen who lived their entire lives next to each other and knew one another inside and out.

And there, in the garden of Gethsemane, it only took two words to pierce their story and splinter history for the rest of time.

*Greetings, Rabbi ...*
**MATTHEW 26:49**

OT   Psalm 41:9

And with that, one of Christ's closest friends kisses the face he has looked at many times, the face of the man he's walked alongside for years.

But Christ loves him. He knows him. He remembers him. He has always known that in this moment He would use these words in response:

*"Friend*, do what you came to do."

Chaos ensues. Swords are out. People are swinging at each other and screaming orders. The disciples run away, leaving Jesus alone with His captors in a moment that will define His ministry.

As they pinned Jesus' hands behind His back, pushed Him forward like an animal, and celebrated His capture, I can't help but wonder if somewhere a few feet away, Judas watched with hot tears on his cheeks.

Judas had asked the chief priests how much they would pay him to reveal where Jesus was hiding, and they tossed thirty pieces of silver at him.

The same amount as the price of a slave.

OT

Exodus 21:32

It wouldn't be until the next morning that Judas would fully realize what he had done. He tried to return the money to the chief priests, telling them he had sinned and betrayed innocent blood.

They refuse it, and Judas throws it into the temple, knowing that the sound of silver hitting the floor will be one of the last sounds he ever hears.

Within minutes, he is hanging by a noose he knotted out of unbearable grief and regret.

Will you lean in with me? I want you to feel the night air and watch the Messiah as He is dragged away.

Since the beginning, there have been echoes of God's voice that find their culmination in the life of Jesus.

Once again, I'll remind you that the sound of His voice wasn't muted by hundreds of years—that was just the amount of time that passed before the Old Testament prophecies were fulfilled by Jesus.

> *Then I said to them, "If it seems good to you, give me my wages; but if not, keep them." And they weighed out as my wages thirty pieces of silver. Then the LORD said to me, "Throw it to the potter"—the lordly price at which I was priced by them. So I took the thirty pieces of silver and threw them into the house of the LORD, to the potter.*
> ZECHARIAH 11:12-13

DAY 4
# THE TRIALS

Before we get going on this one, go back to Week 2, Day 1, and refresh your memory about who is who and what is what.

After Jesus was dragged out of the garden of Gethsemane, He finds Himself face-to-face with a group you'll remember learning about.

&ast; *Read Matthew 26:57-68. Who is Jesus taken to?*

&ast; *Who is the head of this group?*

&ast; *What is his name?*

&ast; *In verse 59, what does it say they are seeking?*

Awesome. Well, you can't say it isn't fair and unbiased, can you?

Several witnesses come forward, and while Jesus listens to their claims, He stays completely silent. He doesn't defend Himself or criticize those who have come before the council to lie about Him.

&ast; *One of the witnesses recalled a statement that Jesus had made. What was it (v. 61)?*

This seems to be a snapping point for Caiaphas, who demands an answer.

&ast; *What does he ask Jesus?*

> He was oppressed, and he was afflicted, yet he opened not his mouth; like a lamb that is led to the slaughter, and like a sheep that before its shearers is silent, so he opened not his mouth.
> **ISAIAH 53:7**

## TIME LINE OF JESUS' TRIALS

1. He is taken first to Annas, who is a former high priest and father-in-law of Caiaphas (John 18:12-14,19-24).
2. Next they send Jesus to the house of Caiaphas, current high priest (Luke 22:54,63-65).
3. Then He's put on trial before the whole Sanhedrin (Luke 22:66-71).
4. The Sanhedrin send Him to Pilate (Luke 23:1-5).
5. And Pilate sends Him to Herod Antipas (Luke 23:6-12).
6. Finally, Herod sends Jesus back to Pilate (Luke 23:11-25).

*Are You?*

The crowds are silent, waiting for the words that they think will end His life once and for all.

*You have said I am.*

He cannot be cornered, and it sends the high priest into a rage. He rips his robe (which is actually forbidden by rabbinic law), and the men begin to spit on Jesus' face and ridicule Him. While Jesus is being questioned, something else is going on.

\* *Read Luke 22:54-62. Describe Peter's experience.*

And Peter, sweet Peter, despite his insistence, denies his association with Jesus three times. After the third denial, a rooster reminds him of the Lord's words. (More on Peter next week. Don't worry, his story is not over.)

After they have mocked and beaten Jesus, they take Him to someone whose name you probably recognize.

\* *Read Matthew 27:1-2. Who is Pontius Pilate?*

\* *Is he a Roman or an Israelite?*

\* *Why do the Sanhedrin need to get him involved?*

Take a step back to make sure you understand this event the same way they would have been experiencing it in the moment.

Ahhhh. And herein lies the problem: the Jews are not permitted to put someone to death. Pontius Pilate is. (Remember? I told you that would matter.)

All they have to do is convince him that Jesus needs to be crucified, but it's not going to be as easy as it seems.

Pilate asks the Jews what Jesus has done, and their answers don't satisfy him. There appears to be no legitimate reason to put Jesus to death.

*Read Mark 15:4-5. How does Jesus respond to Pilate's questioning?*

Remember, Pontius Pilate has one job: to make sure this random guy isn't a threat to Rome. I imagine the answer was fairly obvious based on the state Jesus is in.

*If you were one of the Jews fighting for Pilate to allow them to murder the man claiming to be the Christ, how do you think you would have appealed to him?*

OT    Isaiah 53:7

*He might look innocent, but He's not. His name has spread like wildfire and the number of His followers is growing every day. And also, Pilate? He is telling them to rebel against Rome.*

*What do the Sanhedrin guys tell him in Luke 23:2?*

He is _____, _____ _____.

Wait, what? The Jewish council is calling Rome their nation? Interesting.

*Who do they say Jesus is preventing them from giving tribute to?*

*They tell Pilate that Jesus won't let them pay taxes to Rome. He is claiming to be the _____ _____ _____ _____ (Luke 23:3).*

Pilate doesn't know what to do. The Jews have a clever response when Pilate tells them he finds no fault in Jesus.

*Read Luke 23:5.*

Pilate wants no part of this. As he considers the implications of this decision, he realizes he may not have to be the one who deals with it.

✳ *Read Luke 23:5-7. What does Pilate ask, and why does that matter?*

Wait. Jesus was from Herod's territory? Perfect. I can pass my problem over to him.

Well, well, well, how the tables have turned.

Herod. The king who murdered Jesus' cousin John and ordered his head on a platter to please his stepdaughter and wife.

Herod. The son of the king who tried to have Jesus murdered as a child.

My little bird … it's now time for me to let you fly a little bit. I'm handing over the reins for a second because I believe in you. Ready?

✳ *Read Luke 23:6-16.*

I'm in tears over here. I'm celebrating you. See? You didn't even need help! You understood what was happening, didn't you? Go ahead and write something in the margin. Anything. Just whatever you're thinking. Fly, birdie, fly!

Janet, you and I both know you wrote, "Don't forget to make a dentist appointment for Anna-Sarah-Grace-James and Addie-Gail-Margaret" just to spite me.

Pilate tells the crowd that he will beat Jesus and then release Him. But they are relentless. He will die one way or another.

In Matthew 27:15-23, we read about a Jewish custom: every Passover the governor (Pilate, at the time) chooses one man to be released from prison.

Pontius Pilate gives them two choices: the notorious murderer Barabbas or the Man who says He is the Christ.

*Who do you choose to release?*

*Barabbas!!!!! Barabbas!!!!*

Barabbas was likely being held nearby, and I wonder if he heard the crowds screaming his name. Their voices echoed throughout the bare prison cell as he awaited his fate.

*What do you want me to do with the Christ?*

*Crucify Him! Crucify Him!* the crowd screams.

And Pilate relents.

I imagine Barabbas heard the crowd but not Pilate and assumed he was going to be executed. Surely as the guards made their way to him, he had already accepted the cross he would carry.

What Barabbas wasn't expecting was for someone to unlock the door and tell him he was a free man.

He didn't deserve life; he deserved to die, and he knew it. As he walked into the fresh air, still in shock from what had just happened, I'm sure he heard the commotion and went to see what it was all about.

And there was the Son of Man with a crown of thorns piercing His skin.

Neither Barabbas nor the people knew what had actually happened, nor did they know they had just been witnesses to a great exchange: the innocent will die to free the guilty.

Barabbas was spared, but only because the true Lamb was taking his place.

Many of them had walked hundreds of miles to come to the temple for Passover.

They had come to celebrate the way God passed over them, rescuing them from slavery by a lamb's blood on their wooden doorposts.

As the crowd applauds the cruel mocking and unmistakable sound of whips splitting Jesus' skin open, they taunt Him. And they never knew that as the soldiers pressed the thorns deeper into His human flesh, they are actually crowning the true King.

DAY 5
# THE CRUCIFIXION

And with that, the Son of God began His walk to Calvary with a beam of wood across His back. He had lost so much blood that it was nearly impossible for Him to bear the weight without staggering, each step more agonizing than the last.

Simon was from Cyrene, part of present-day Tripoli. He was probably a Jew who had come to Jerusalem for the Passover.

A stranger along the road was ordered to help Jesus carry His cross. Of course Simon, a man who had likely traveled from Cyrene for the Passover, had no idea that he was walking alongside the true Christ as Jesus walked toward His death.

I wonder if He heard the cries of His mother. Jesus could no longer feel her arms around Him; He could no longer experience a mother's comfort.

As they reached Golgotha, "The Place of a Skull" (John 19:17), Jesus watched as the soldiers prepared His cross. Above His head was a sign that Pilate had requested: *This is Jesus, King of the Jews.*

The Jews were furious and insisted that Pilate change the words.

Isaiah 53    OT

It should say, "He *said* He was the king of the Jews," they screamed.

Pilate refused to change it.

*"What I have written I have written" (John 19:22).*

The soldiers stood around the cross, planning out what they would take from Jesus. They split everything up into four shares, but one thing remained.

＊ *What was it (John 19:23-24)?*

＊ *What was interesting about this particular garment?*

＊ *What did they decide to do to determine who it went to?*

*Now turn back to Psalm 22:17-18. What does it say will happen to the Savior's clothes?

*What happens in Matthew 27:34?

This drink was intended to dull some of the pain Jesus would feel, but at this point He refused it in order to take the full weight of death and sin.

During the process of crucifixion, people would push their feet against the cross to lift their weight. When they were too weak to do that, their bodies slouched, and they typically died of asphyxiation, blood loss, or heart failure. The process of crucifixion could take anywhere from a few hours to several days. If it was the day before the Sabbath (as it was when Jesus was crucified), the soldiers would typically break the legs of the men who were still alive later in the day in order to speed up the process, as they weren't allowed to remove the bodies on the Sabbath.

*"Father, forgive them, for they know not what they do" (Luke 23:34).*

Jesus has been with them. He has eaten meals with them and walked their dusty roads. He knows what it's like to love them in His humanity—just the way anyone else would. And He has loved them—every one of them. Every one of us.

He knew what it felt like to be among them.

And yet they laughed at Him and mocked Him: *He should be able to save Himself if He is God, right?*

*I thirst ...*

He knew what it felt like to have a need.

A stranger in the crowd offered Him a sponge full of wine.

Hung between two criminals, Jesus acknowledges that one of them believes in Him.

*"Truly, I say to you, today you will be with me in paradise" (Luke 23:43).*

He knew what it felt like to look into the face of His children.

And there, close enough to hear her Son but not close enough to touch Him, was His mother. All she could do was watch helplessly as the thorns pressed into His forehead and His bruises began to change color.

Some scholars believe they know where Christ was crucified; it's a small hill outside the city with an unmistakable image of a skull in the rocks. **GOLGOTHA.**

She used to scratch the back they are whipping.

She brushed His hair before school—just where that crown is cutting.

She sees the nails—pushing through the hands she held and the feet that first learned to walk to her.

There were a few people near the cross that day who had loved Him and believed He was who He said He was.

But not one of them could have known what Mary did. No one could possibly know what she did; not in the same way. He is the One we have been waiting for.

It's all true.

*"Woman, behold, your son!" Then he said to the disciple, "Behold, your mother!" (John 19:26-27).*

He knew what it felt like for her to kiss His face.

But relationships would be defined differently now. They are bound together by faith, and His role in her life is changing.

He isn't her Son in the same way.

He is the Son of God—the God He cannot find for the moment.

*"My God, my God, why have you forsaken me?" (Mark 15:34).*

He had never known what it felt like to
be separated from His Father.

He calls out in desperation.

It is the only time on earth Jesus doesn't call Him Father. In that moment, He feels like He is no one's Son. He feels abandoned by His Father as He is crucified by the very people He came to save.

Will He rescue Himself?

Psalm 22:7-8
Psalm 69:21

OT

No, He won't.

He will stay in order to rescue them—to rescue us.

There is no way to find the words to describe the agony He must have felt. We can't begin to understand, but we can't forget that it happened.

Every sin. Not just for yesterday. For today and every day that will come.

As Jesus surrenders to His Father, He speaks only a few words. He cried out with a loud voice and then spoke some of His final words:

*"Father, into Your hands I commit my spirit"* (Luke 23:46).

*"It is finished"* (John 19:30).

He shouted and then took His last breath.

He knew what it was like to surrender His will.

He fulfilled all of the prophecies of a coming Savior. He lived a perfect life for us because we never could.

The sky had gone dark, and the sun failed to shine. At that moment, the ground shook and rocks split.

Historians have noted that there was an extraordinary eclipse of the sun on this day.[8] They said the stars in heaven could be seen and that an earthquake shook the world.

The Lamb was slain on our behalf. He was the sacrifice that would rescue those who believe. He atoned for our sins, not just temporarily but permanently. We are covered by His blood, forgiven by His mercy, and loved by His grace.

Hundreds of years before this, hyssop branches were raised to paint blood over His children's doors. During His crucifixion, He watched a sponge of wine being placed on a hyssop branch and raised to His mouth.

*Pass over us.*

But this time it wasn't just for the Jews.

While the sky was dark and the ground was trembling, something else happened.

A great sound echoed from inside the temple.

It was the sound of a seamless curtain being torn in half from top to bottom—from heaven to earth—nevermore to separate us from God through the gift of our one true Passover Lamb.

The phrase, "It is finished," is one word in Greek—*tetelestai*.[6] The term was also found on ancient tax receipts, meaning "paid in full."[7]

seven

WEEK 7

# PROMISE: THE RISEN LORD

Here's what I love about this week. The Son of God didn't just come back from the dead, wait for applause, and disappear. He spent time with His followers. These biblical accounts give us an imaginary seat at the table to see how Jesus spent time with His disciples and other followers over this last forty-day period.

He didn't make His resurrection a big secret or mystery, but He wasn't posting about it on social media either. (Is it just me or do you feel like the whole, "I came back to life" thing feels like a draw? I mean the rumor that He was dead a couple of days ago would have probably been enough to pack out stadiums. But that's not what He was about. Just like Jesus to come back from the dead and still fly under the radar.) He just walked right on back into His life and spent time with the people who needed Him. I guess this seems like a detail worth mentioning, because the Bible tells us it was more than just a handful of guys He knew during His life who could claim to have seen Him.

Every stop He made on this farewell tour had a purpose—to teach, to restore, to challenge. (Of course, that makes sense considering Jesus always had a purpose for everything—and still does, for that matter.) He knew His time on earth was nearly done. And, as any good leader does during his swan song, Jesus was handing over the reigns of ministry to His followers, saying a "see you later" to the people He loved so dearly. He reassured them that He would send the Holy Spirit to help finish what He had started.

Jesus had several meaningful interactions that give us a glimpse into what life looked like on the other side of the tomb, reinforcing His tenderness and dedication in such personal ways. We see Him eating with friends; no one grills a fireside fish brunch quite like Jesus. We see Him journeying with skeptical followers on the road to Emmaus. We see Him turning a foe into a follower.

In these fleeting forty days, Jesus prioritized people. He didn't want to leave the mission unclear or relationships undone. It seems He especially had an eye to reach the doubter and denier, those who might be harder to love. (Not that any of us would know anything about that.) It's one thing for Jesus to tell His followers how much He loves them before they abandon Him, but it's another thing entirely for Him to come back with evidence of the wounds He bore for them.

None of us can fathom a world where we would be forgiven after such shameful behavior, let alone be loved in spite of it.

It helps us understand the heart of the narrative we've followed since the beginning: Jesus refuses to stop loving us, even when we don't know how to love Him in return.

## GROUP SESSION GUIDE

SESSION 7: REVIEW WEEK 6 HOMEWORK

* What new things did you grasp from the Scripture this week in your homework?

* Day 1: Why is Jesus' fulfillment of all the Old Testament prophecies about the Messiah such a big deal?

* What was the significance of Jesus' triumphal entry into Jerusalem? And why ride in on a donkey? Why was that important?

* Day 2: What was the meaning of the Passover and how did Jesus change the meaning of it? What did Jesus say was the significance of the bread and the juice? Will what you learned on this day of study affect the way you view the Lord's Supper? Why or why not?

* Day 3: When Jesus was arrested in the garden, all the disciples ran away. It's easy to look down on them for abandoning Jesus, but do you think you would have acted any differently? In what situations do you tend to separate yourself from Jesus?

* Day 4: When Jesus was led to trial, Peter followed at a distance. He ended up denying Christ three times. What bold predictions or promises have you made to the Lord that you didn't follow through on?

✻ Day 5: As you have watched this story of Jesus' walk to the cross unfold, what are your emotions and thoughts? Have you read and heard the story so much that you're numb to the suffering? Or does it move you when you realize all Jesus has done for you? Explain.

**WATCH SESSION 7 (VIDEO RUN TIME: 12:00)**

## DISCUSS

✻ What part of the video spoke to you the most? Why?

✻ Do you feel like you live ready to give a reason for the hope that is within you? Are you always ready to share the gospel? Why or why not? What gives you pause?

✻ What does Angie mean when she says she doesn't want people to ever feel like a project? Why is building a relationship with someone so important when it comes to sharing your faith? How have you experienced this?

✻ How are you and your church working to continue Jesus' ministry in your community and around the world?

Video sessions available for purchase or rent
at *LifeWay.com/Matchless*

DAY 1
# RESURRECTION

Jesus offered Himself as a sacrifice, as an atonement for the sins of the world. He fulfilled every prophecy in order for the world to believe in His Father. Everything He did was to bring glory to God, and it didn't stop when He died.

\* Read John 19:31-33. Since Jesus was already dead, what was unnecessary for them to do?

\* Find Psalm 34:20 and write down what the prophecy says.

\* What happens in John 19:34?

One of the soldiers _____ his side with a spear, and _____ and _____ flowed out immediately.

\* Now find Zechariah 12:10 and write it down.

Beautiful. Just beautiful. And this next part? I never understood it before I was writing this study. I love this kind of stuff.

\* Read Mark 15:42-47. Who requests the body of Jesus?

\* What is he going to do with Jesus' body?

\* Don't miss this, friend. What detail about Joseph is tucked into verse 43?

*These are the kinds of sentences we might have skipped over before, and we would have missed the significance of six small words that change the way we understand what is happening: "Joseph of Arimathea, a _____ _____ _____ _____ council."*

Joseph was part of the Sanhedrin—the group who had fought to have Jesus crucified.

It appears that he didn't agree with the decision, and he is obviously someone who cares greatly for what will now happen with Christ's body.

*Typically, bodies were left on the cross to rot, but there is a problem. What is it? (See Mark 15:42.)*

The Jewish Sabbath was from sundown on Friday to sundown on Saturday.

The last thing they wanted to do was leave a body hanging on a cross while throngs of people were still in Jerusalem—not exactly something to highlight in the Jerusalem Visitor's Bureau brochure. The day after Jesus died was the Sabbath, so they wouldn't be able to do the work of removing His body.

*Who are we told is standing near the cross where Jesus died (John 19:25)?*

Are you ready for this? There was one other person who helped to physically remove the Savior from His cross.

*Who is it? Do you remember him? Read John 19:39.*

Isn't that beautiful? The Pharisee who came to Jesus humbly because he wanted to understand true salvation. I wonder if he was thinking about the words Christ had spoken over him that night—the very words we cling to as the bride of Christ.

*For God so loved the world, that he gave his only Son, that whoever believes in him should not perish but have eternal life (John 3:16).*

We know they have been given Christ's body, but we can't take a step toward the tomb until we sit here first. The disciples have abandoned Him. It seems everyone has abandoned Him.

The only people bold enough to ask for the body of the Lamb were two Pharisees who both held prominent positions on the Jewish council.

Now can we head to the tomb? Not yet. We haven't seen the hardest part.

Think about the fact that Nicodemus and Joseph physically took Jesus off the cross. They must have used a ladder to reach Him, and when they did, they would have been touching the ripped flesh and bruised body of the Man they loved.

It wasn't an easy feat to remove someone who was hanging the way Christ was. His hands—nailed all the way through His wrists—probably had to be hammered from the back and pulled from the front. They would do the same with His feet, trying to balance Him, speaking to one another about how they should proceed. His knees had buckled when He died, and His body had slipped, no longer held up by His feet. He was mangled. Unrecognizable. Swollen, bruised, and lifeless. They saw His eyes closed and His mouth motionless.

They are bearing the weight of the Man who had just borne the weight of their sin. They struggled, no doubt. They must have wept while they worked together, this time not as part of the council that condemned Him but as brothers in Christ. Once He had been released from the cross, they wrapped Him in linen cloths as a preparation for burial. There wasn't time to do it properly, so the required spices weren't applied to His body before the shroud was.

You remember who was watching, right?

Mary, mother of Jesus.

The one who could no longer see enough of her Son's flesh to identify Him.

Mary, mother of Jesus.

The one who taught Him how to pick up His food and held His hand while they walked to the temple.

Mary, mother of Jesus.

The Boy who she had swaddled as a Baby, now swaddled in strips of cloth.

Remember when we talked about the shepherds who were the first to see Jesus? The ones who raised the sacrificial lambs?

Obviously perfect lambs need to be well cared for, protected and kept from anything that would blemish them. Can you imagine trying to keep a baby lamb calm while all it wants to do is wiggle and kick? If you've only got one, you might be al lright, but that's not the case here. Only one shepherd and a herd of sheep—there has to be a better solution that will keep them all safe.

Which, I suppose, is the reason the sacrificial lambs are swaddled the moment they are born.

DAY 2
# RESPONSE

If the resurrection hadn't happened, the whole thing would have been a sham. It's what showed the world that Jesus is who He says He is and had fulfilled the assignment that was given to Him.

He told them He was coming back in three days, and that statement made the chief priests and Pharisees nervous.

> \* Read Matthew 27:62-66. What action did the religious leaders take?

They assumed the disciples were going to steal His body and pretend He had come back to life, so Pilate gave them a guard of soldiers to help seal the stone and stand around the tomb the entire time to make sure that wasn't possible.

*Turns out somehow they missed the part where the stone did move (YOU HAD ONE JOB), so the elders told them to lie and say the disciples took Him while they were sleeping.*

Evidently, Pilate did not send his light sleepers.

Before the sun came up on Sunday, Mary Magdalene went to Jesus' tomb and saw the stone rolled away from the entrance.

> \* What did she think had happened to Him (John 20:1-2)?

The women brought spices not to embalm Jesus, because that was not something Jews did. Instead, the spices were intended to reduce the smell of the decomposing body.[1]

Peter and John rush to the tomb, not quite sure what they are going to see. As they stare into the darkness where the Lord had been, they were shocked at what was left behind.

> \* Read John 20:4-7 and describe what they saw.

It's not exactly what I would have pictured. I mean, do body-robbers often fold laundry before dragging out the dead person? Want to hear something beautiful? Some believe that there was a Jewish tradition during that time that involved a master and his slave. After the slave set the table for his master, he was to move out of sight until the master indicated that he was finished. If the master stood, wiped his face, and left his napkin crumpled on the table, it meant that he was done and the servant was free to clean up. If, however, the man stood but left the napkin folded neatly, he was indicating that he would be coming back.[2]

Peter and John don't know what to make of the whole thing, so they head home, but Mary stays by the empty tomb and weeps for Jesus.

* *Read John 20:11-13. When Mary Magdalene looks in, what does she see? How does she respond to their question?*

This is the Man who rescued her from demon possession, the Man she watched take His last breaths. She was devoted and consistent in her walk with Christ.

She turns when she hears the same words again, "Woman, why are you weeping?" (v. 15).

Supposing that the man was the gardener, she told him that if he was the one who had taken the body, she would go retrieve Him. She just wants to find the body of her beloved Christ.

And then she hears one word: *Mary.*

Instantly she knows the Man is her Lord. She calls Him *Rabboni* (teacher) and then follows His instructions to tell the disciples.

During this time period, the testimony of women was essentially useless. It wasn't considered worthy of listening to because of the place a woman had in society. So once again Jesus uses the least likely person for the most important task. Naturally, the fellas didn't believe her and thought it sounded like a fairy tale (Luke 24:9-11).

It should be noted here that, as often is the case in Scripture, the Gospels tell slightly different versions of how the empty tomb was found and exactly what happened after that.

Regardless, the most pertinent detail is consistent: the tomb is empty. Jesus has opened His eyes in victory and returned to life in order to defeat death and prove He is the Son of God.

The disciples are hiding because they are afraid of what the Jews would do to them. I'm pretty sure they weren't expecting their next house guest.

Jesus appears in the flesh, telling them to be at peace and not be afraid about Him being there.

That sounds perfectly reasonable.

He invites them to look at His wounds and reminds them that a spirit doesn't have bones. He is a real man, and He had real requests.

The next thing Jesus asked was, "Do you have anything here to eat?" (Luke 24:41, CSB).

He is a Man after my own Italian heart. I mean, I don't blame Him—I bet being dead for three days makes you hangry.

They give Him a piece of fish, and He proceeds to eat it in front of them. Isn't it funny that some of the details in these stories seem so random? Do we need to know He ordered food?

*What reason would make this an important part of
   the narrative?*

Well, hopefully you picked up on the fact that He is reiterating that He is in a body that could walk, eat, talk, and so forth, as He had before.

*Also, I think this part is kind of interesting.
   Find Mark 16:14. What was He rebuking them for?*

OK, let me get this straight. He is hanging out with the people who abandoned Him in the most horrifying hours of His life. They have lied about knowing Him, denied Him, and doubted Him.

And He never says a word about it. As far as He is concerned, it's done and gone. He could have walked in and condemned them or cried over their fickle commitment, but instead He tells them they should have believed He was alive.

*Take a look at Luke 24:44-49. You'll never guess which kind of party is about to get started up in here—a fill-in-the-blank party!*

*Then he said to them, "These are my words that I spoke to you while I was still with you, that everything written about me in the Law of _____ and the _____ and the _____ must be fulfilled."*

Quick interruption for a word from our sponsor. OH MY GOODNESS, WE KNOW WHAT HE IS TALKING ABOUT. And back to the show.

And with that, we transition to what is commonly referred to as the "Great Commission."

*Let's go to Matthew 28:16-20. What is Jesus commissioning us to do as His followers?*

Before Jesus returned to His Father, He promised His disciples (including us) that He would always be here—that He will never leave us for a single moment. None. Not one moment.

They didn't understand that He was talking about the Holy Spirit because they had no concept of how He could be with them when He wasn't actually with them.

Don't worry. He has a plan for that.

We're talking about a bunch of disciples we'll never meet and conversations we'll never hear. It sounds far away and disconnected sometimes.

What we have to remember is that those words meet us exactly where we are and speak the same commission over us.

It's so easy to keep Scripture at arm's length, I know. But if you listen carefully, you'll hear your name in this story. How?

Just listen for your Shepherd.

You'll recognize His voice.

DAY 3
# ROAD TO EMMAUS

As they walked the dusty road toward Emmaus, the two men talked about all the things that had happened and considered what they meant.

They were only a few miles away from their destination when a man caught up with them. In true form, Jesus didn't force His thoughts or opinions.

> \* Let's take a look at the story. Read Luke 24:13-18. How does Jesus approach them?

> \* What is the first thing Jesus says to them?
> A question. Just a simple question. What is it?

*Hey, fellas. What's going on? You look really serious. Also, I know I'm a complete stranger who just interrupted your conversation, but now can you tell me about Myself? Great. Thanks.*

> \* How did the two disciples respond?

*Dude, this is literally the only thing anyone has been talking about. How on earth have you not heard?*

Jesus plays it cool. *Heard what?*

This is obviously not the case, but it makes me think about the way my husband tries to sneakily bring up something because he wants to be acknowledged and complimented. "What did you mean when you said I was awesome?"

*Ohhhh, stop. Don't say another word abo …* never mind. Let's keep this thing going.

Evidently these two travelers were followers of Jesus. They were numbered with "all the rest" in Luke 24:9.

*Read Luke 24:19-24.

These guys are going deep, aren't they?

Verse 21 is where I stop every time.

*We hoped He was the One who was going to redeem Israel.*

*We thought He was the One we had been waiting for. Everything lined up. Everyone had been talking about Him because we thought … well … we thought He was our Redeemer. It's the third day since He died, and He said that He would come back to life by now.*

They recount the fact that people have seen an empty tomb, but they are distressed and obviously don't believe He had risen from the dead.

Boys, you're going to have a crazy night so buckle up. Also, you're not going to like the stranger's response.

*Read Luke 24:25-27 and summarize what Jesus said.*


This is what we call NOT VAGUE.

As we read the words, it sounds like He's basically calling them idiots. *Why don't you believe it's true? Christ had to suffer so you could have eternal life. I had to … He had to suffer.*

And this is where I say what you're thinking: *Yes. Yes, it does sound like* Mrs. Doubtfire *and* Undercover Boss *have collaborated, and this was the first episode.*

Christ doesn't allow them to recognize who He is. I love the part where it says, "he interpreted to them in all the Scriptures the things concerning himself" (v. 27).

Jesus starts with Moses. (How long is this road trip? Who starts with MOSES?)

I think you know the answer.

Despite the fact that He has dominated their bro-time with stories from the Book of Exodus, they still think He'll be a good hang, so they ask Him to stay for supper.

*There must have been something about Him.*

It was a humble home and a humble meal. To them, it was an ordinary dinner.

Once again, He went to their territory, making Himself a part of their world and speaking to them in ways He knew they would understand.

We don't know how long they talked, but we do know when the big reveal happened.

*Read verses 30-31.*

*Surpriiiissssseee! It's Me!*

And then He disappeared. Which is obviously super bizarre because who disappears before eating a meal? Not me, I'll tell you that much.

I wonder what He looked like at that moment and what it was that made them realize it was Him. Did they see His wounds? It seems unlikely that a few men out of thousands and thousands of people would recognize His face.

They immediately head toward Jerusalem and find the disciples talking about the fact that Jesus has been spotted.

They tell the disciples that it's true—they saw Him for themselves.

*He just broke the bread, and we knew it was Him! It was the craziest thing! But then He kind of disappeared, so we didn't get a chance to ask Him about the being dead thing.*

Did the bread just hover in the air and fall down when He left? Did He ask for a to-go box?

And surely they knew the way God had provided manna in the desert.

They must have heard how Jesus fed five thousand people by breaking a few small pieces of bread.

And they knew about the first Passover, the way the Israelites had to eat unleavened bread so they could quickly escape the Egyptians.

*Give us this day our daily bread.*

*This is My body, which is given for you.*

*Read John 6:32-35 and summarize what it is saying.*

When Jesus ate with rich people, He probably would have eaten white bread. But most of the time He probably ate bread made from barley. The bread of the poor.[3]

It was never Moses. It wasn't Noah, Abraham, Jacob, Isaac, or John the Baptist.

It is God who provides.

For sustenance.

For a sign of provision.

For remembrance of the way He rescued us.

He was born in Bethlehem, which, remember, means "House of bread."[4]

> *Go to John 6:48-51, and remember that this is long before the last supper. Jesus is teaching in a synagogue, where the people are surely confused about what He is saying.

Little did they know that He was telling them that life would come from His death, and the breaking would be necessary. The Bread of life, broken for them.

> *Go to Deuteronomy 8:3. Remember that these words are from the speeches given as the Israelites are about to enter the promised land. They are words that would have been handed down to them through Moses in order to remind them of the way God had saved and sent them.

> Man does not live by _____ _____, but by

> _____ _____ _____ _____ _____

> _____ _____ _____ _____ _____.

And for those who believe that He is who He says He is, there will be a great banquet in heaven. We will sit with our Lord Jesus as the bread of the new kingdom is broken.

Until then, we wait with the hope that comes from experiencing Him and knowing that He is the One who made the Scriptures come to life, burning in our hearts and making us long to be with Him.

Immediately, the men ran to the eleven disciples and told them exactly what had happened.

*He was with us. We don't know where He is now, but we know we saw Him.*

*The footsteps you have followed for the last three years belong to the Messiah, and we saw Him long enough to believe.*

DAY 4
# RESTORATION

The simplified version of the life of Christ is this: He came to earth to rescue us from our sin, and by acknowledging that He is God and repenting, we will become one with Him and one day join Him in heaven.

No matter how many times I've tried to write that with softer edges, it just won't budge. It still sounds like church language. Not that there is anything wrong with that (it's how the gospel was given to us in the Bible), but when I hear *repent*, my mind goes to a God who is forcing me into submission. To be abundantly clear, Janet, I know that is not what the word means, but I'm allowed to have my own responses.

In the event that you've ever been intimidated by language used in Scripture and in frequent church conversations, let me share what has really helped for me.

If you look up the original Greek word for *repent* (as you do), you will see that a more accurate version of the translation shows up. "To change one's mind for better ... to reconsider."[5] To recognize the magnitude of our past sin.

> Or do you despise the riches of his kindness, restraint, and patience, not recognizing that God's kindness is intended to lead you to repentance?
> **ROMANS 2:4, CSB**

For clarification, there's a tremendous weight and responsibility in asking for forgiveness from the Lord. It's not to be taken lightly or flippantly. But I also know that a lot of people hear the word and their first thought is, *I'm going to go to hell if I don't repent*, before they think, *God has given me the opportunity to realize I've made terrible choices, but it isn't too late for me to change my mind for the better.*

  \* *Does this resonate at all with you? In what ways?*

There are a few stories in Scripture that have always moved me in ways that remind me of the tenderness of God and the way He loves us when we come to Him in confession.

Two of these stories happen after Jesus has been resurrected and is going back to see His disciples (you know, around the time He was craving fish).

*Turn to John 20 and read verses 24-25. Summarize what's happening in the space below.*

Quick question here: Do you think God knew Thomas wasn't going to be there? I'm not going to leave a space. I'm pretty sure you got this one right.

Thomas is pretty stubborn, but for the record, he was actually a loyal and committed disciple during Christ's life (John 11:1-16).

In my opinion, Thomas isn't making his statements based on the fact that he was full of doubt about what the disciples were telling him; I think he doubted because he wanted so much to believe.

About a week passes with no sign of the resurrected Christ.

The only thing Thomas has to go on is other people's testimony. But they aren't exactly normal "other people." They are folks he had traveled with for three years while closely following Jesus.

*What does Jesus say when He appears to Thomas (20:26-27)?*

Incidentally, Jesus wasn't there when Thomas made those demands, so the fact that He addresses Thomas' three requirements for belief is significant.

There's something I want to point out about this interaction. In verse 27, we see a few words strung together that speak directly to who Christ is and how He chooses to approach us in our doubt.

"Then he said to Thomas ..."

Five words that remind us Jesus doesn't come after us with blame, accusations, or shame when we have doubted. In fact, He turns His head in our direction and looks us in the eye, offering up His consolation instead of His condemnation.

We don't have any reason to believe Thomas ever touched Christ, but we have every reason to believe he didn't have to in order to believe.

*What does Thomas call Jesus in verse 28?*

This is the first time in all of Scripture that Jesus is referred to as Lord and God, and it was spoken by the one we still think of as the doubter.

\* *What's the next thing Jesus says to Thomas (v. 29)?*

He's essentially saying the same thing He did earlier when He rebuked the disciples in Mark 16:14: *Do you have to see Me to believe in Me? Will you not accept the testimony of others?*

At no point during this interaction do we hear Thomas rattle off the list of sins he can recall from the past few days while explaining that he is repenting and asking for forgiveness.

In fact, not one person apologizes to Christ in the Gospels.

There are a few people who cry out for Jesus to have mercy on them, but every single instance is related to physical healing, not necessarily repentance. And when Jesus says the words, *your sins are forgiven*, He's usually speaking to someone He has just healed of a physical ailment. There's one notable exception: the prostitute who has come to anoint His feet with oil (Luke 7:48).

As you may recall, her only identification in the Bible is as "a sinner," and despite the fact that we never hear her utter a single word, Jesus forgives her because of her faith (v. 50).

There is another beautiful story of forgiveness in the New Testament that's worth us spending a few minutes on, and it occurs immediately after the story of Thomas.

\* *Read John 21:1-19 and answer these questions.*

\* *What does Jesus ask the disciples before they realize who He is (v. 5)?*

\* *What does He tell them to do next, and what happens when they obey?*

\* *After John tells Peter that it's the Lord speaking, what does Peter do?*

*What do the other disciples do?*

I just think it's funny that the risen Christ is standing on the shoreline and they're like, *Well, we better get all these fish to shore because I can't see any way we could catch this many again!*

*What do they see when they get back on land?*

Jesus invites them to a breakfast meal of fish, and the disciples didn't have to ask Him who He was, which is progress in the right direction as far as I'm concerned.

*After they eat, Jesus begins to speak to Simon. Read verses 15-17. What did Jesus ask Peter? How many times did He ask?*

*What did He instruct Peter to do after he answered Him?*

*Now flip back a couple of pages to John 18 and read verses 15-18 and 25-27. How many times did Peter deny knowing Jesus?*

*What was Peter standing next to when he denied Christ?*

This wasn't an accident; Jesus had set the scene as reminiscent of the setting where Peter had denied Him. Don't you think as Jesus asked the three questions Peter recalled his three denials?

Jesus wasn't trying to be cruel or taunt Peter with his past mistakes. He simply wanted Peter to remember and be restored.

Our repentance isn't based on us getting all the words right or recounting every single sin we've committed; it's the recognition that when we turn to Jesus, He does what He does best: forgive.

## DAY 5
# RETURN OF CHRIST

The Trinity (also known as the Triune God) is the Father, Son, and Holy Spirit. They aren't three separate entities, but they are each distinct Persons. They are the same Being. God. They are all God.

What I'm trying to say is that I join the hundreds of thousands of believers who have also gotten a little tongue-tied when they've tried to explain this stuff.

At the risk of sounding like I'm trying to dodge the question, let me be clear: I'm trying to dodge the question. Let's talk about Revelation instead.

The truth is that it's humanly impossible for us to wrap our brains around the idea of a God who consists of three that are all one. So I guess I'll correct my above statement: I'm not exactly trying to dodge it so much as I'm trying not to spend a lot of time explaining something that no one can perfectly explain.

Do you know how much I love my husband? The people who know me could answer that question despite the fact that I can't prove that I do.

- "We go on dates sometimes."
- "He's an amazing dad."
- "I can't imagine living without him, and he's the best thing that's ever happened to me."
- "In eighteen years we've never had a single disagreement, nor have I ever slammed ..."

Those are all one hundred percent true. Well, not exactly, but you get the point. I've given you several reasons to believe that I love my husband, but I can never prove to you that's the case.

The Holy Spirit is who enables me to desire Christ, to follow Him, to believe in Him. The Spirit convicts me of my sin. He is also a comfort, an Encourager, a Counselor, and the One who gives me passion and insight for Scripture. Once we become Christians, the Holy Spirit takes up residence in our physical bodies. Please don't ask me to give exact details about the move-in process or how it works once He's there.

Jesus promised that He would send the Holy Spirit.

*Read Acts 2:1-13 and tell me that it doesn't sound like they are hammered by the end of it.*

Don't worry, in the next sentence Peter clarifies that it's not that kind of get-together.

Again, I can't help but smile when Peter explains the reason why they couldn't be drunk because it was only the third hour of the day (about 9 a.m.). I mean, if it was like 5 p.m., this whole theory would be a valid option.

At least he's armed with a solid explanation.

With the sound of rushing wind, the Holy Spirit fell on the people gathered there and filled those believers. But it wasn't just that day and it wasn't just those believers. The same Holy Spirit fills every person who comes to faith in Jesus Christ.

We're flawed and broken. Sometimes we don't know how to pray or act or read or speak or ... well, anything. The Holy Spirit resides in us to guide us, teach us, comfort us, and allow us to have a closer connection to God.

Are you ready for this? Remember way back when the Israelites were working their way through the desert and they kept moving their temporary temple the tabernacle (say that three times fast) around with them?

And then remember when they built a temple? And then had to rebuild it? They did all of this because they believed that the Spirit of God resided there, in the most holy place.

Want to hear something crazy? If you're a believer in Christ, guess what? Your body is now the temple. Yep. True story.

This is the only time I'm going to send you beyond the Gospels. (You're going to be able to read and understand those so much better now. You don't need me.) But I want you to read these words.

*Head to 1 Corinthians 6:19. What does it say?*

But concerning that day and hour no one knows, not even the angels of heaven, nor the Son, but the Father only.
**MATTHEW 24:36**

See? Told you so. And now for the even better news.

One day He will return. (No one knows when, so don't go chasing down all the theories—especially if people are jumping off roofs at midnight on New Year's Eve. That's not a thing. That's an ER visit.) For the record, when Jesus was here on earth He said that even He didn't know the time, only God did. There's that three-in-one thing again. Let it go. You can't fully understand it. God will explain it one day when you meet Him.

When Jesus does return, there are a few things that Scripture says are going to happen. Keep in mind that for the purposes of this study I'm not going to go into an extraordinary amount of detail, but I do want you to know the basics.

I love that I just said I'm going to talk about the basic parts of the second coming of Christ.

I really need to take a CPR class.

 * Read Luke 12:35-40 and summarize what it's talking about in your own words.

We've touched on this before, but now we're going to take it a little further. I'll warn you; it's going to get intense. Don't worry, pet. It has a good ending.

Have you ever heard the verse that says "He will wipe away every tear from their eyes" (Rev. 21:4)? It's used a lot as an encouragement (and it is) in times of grief, but I don't know that people realize He isn't talking about something that will happen in our everyday lives.

Jesus is coming back to claim His bride, but He will also come with fury and fire.

The Lamb will return as a Lion.

 * Read Isaiah 66:15-16.

"Those slain by the Lord shall be many" is referring to those who have not believed in Him, and their punishment is eternity in hell (v. 16b).

There's just not a gentle way to say it, because the text is the text, and the text is true.

God will defeat Satan once and for all, and He will establish "the new heavens and the new earth," where He will sit on the throne and live with His people (Isa. 66:22).

There are about a bazillion more details about His second coming throughout Scripture, but WHOA it's overwhelming. You aren't required

Find out what Jesus Himself said about His second coming in Matthew 24; Mark 13; and Luke 21.

to memorize every detail, but I will tell you something interesting: The Book of Revelation is the only book in the Bible that God promises a blessing for reading it (Rev. 1:3).

It's hard to imagine Christ coming in the clouds in physical form to gather all His people and take us up to be with Him. I mean, it sounds crazy. I get lost in the logistics. Will He fly? Who knows.

But that's (give or take a few details) what He promised to do.

*Jesus Himself said it. Read John 14:1-3 and write His promise.*

Jesus was clear: *I'm going away, but I'm coming back to get you.*

*Read Acts 1:4-11 and describe what happened.*

Jesus didn't leave us with nothing to do. He told His followers to be witnesses, well—everywhere. But He also said we wouldn't do it alone; He would send His Spirit to empower us and to be our guide. (Remember, His Spirit dwells in us as followers of Jesus.)

I can't deny the prophecies about Christ's first coming being true. I see Him in those words, and I believe they were spoken by our Father. And I have to believe the same will be true when He comes again.

So why did this all start with a perfect garden where Eve would reach instead of pulling away? Why did all of it have to happen? I don't understand why God would choose for His Son to be nailed to a cross, and I don't know how He healed people with the touch of His hand. I don't know why animals were sacrificed or why there were prophets and kings. Why? When there were an infinite number of other possibilities, why did He choose this?

*Why did He let my father die?*

After all these weeks, all these stories, we come to our conclusion. As I promised from the beginning, it's probable that we have more questions than answers.

It's OK to ask questions of the God you love. He loves you more in return, and He knows you're human.

He knows what it feels like to live a life like yours.

He knows we grieve for what we don't have here on earth and long for the things we'll have with Him in heaven.

Our Passover Lamb, crucified to atone for our sins.

Our matchless Savior, risen to save us.

*Why would You ever choose me as a daughter?*

This is the exact spot where a good writer would make a perfect transition into the last section of words she's going to say to you, but the truth is that I don't have the perfect words to say. Which may mean I need to check with the 911 center because apparently they think they have more important things to do than review my job application.

The truth is this: we are living in the in-between, the *now* and the *not yet*—with all of its brokenness, shadows, and holy expectation. But we don't do it alone. So how do we press on? I'm not sure, exactly, but I'll tell you how I'm going to try to.

I'm going to wear a white gown with my arm slipped through my father's, not knowing when the door will open, and I will see the One who is waiting.

I'm going to try to live my life with my ear pressed to the church door so I can hear the faint sound of music and the excitement of those who are already there.

I will continue to recognize that the veil of this world makes things look hazy and uncertain, but one day my Father will lift it, and I will see.

I will believe He is there waiting, even though I can't see Him.

I will also remind myself that one day I'll be with Him, and I'll stand back to see the canvas in its entirety, stretched through all of time with the brushstrokes of our lives falling exactly where they were always supposed to be.

I know it's going to be beautiful—more beautiful than I can imagine in my wildest dreams.

There is a lot I won't know in this life; that's just how this works. But I know one thing for sure, and it's what I'll cling to until I don't have to anymore.

I can't remember if I've mentioned this before—maybe so?

In any case, it's true:

*My Father is an amazing Painter.*

eight

WEEK 8
# PERSONAL: A CHOICE TO MAKE

I don't like this day. I refuse to say goodbye, because I don't like the word.

It insinuates that our paths won't cross again, and it feels so final. Here's what I want you to hear me say: this has been one of the most emotional projects I have ever had my name on. You'll never know how often I thought of you as I was writing, or how many times I prayed that my words would not be so loud that they might drown out what Jesus wanted to say.

I wrote this study in a time period that will never exist again, at least I pray it won't. I wrote some of the homework within a half hour of designing my dad's tombstone. I wrote from airplanes that shook in the sky while I cried. I stayed up, woke up, and gave up more times than I can count.

You, my stranger-friend, entered my life when I felt the least equipped to play the part of a Bible teacher.

Which, ironically, I learned was not necessary in order for the gospel to continue to spread—I will tell you THAT WAS SURE A RELIEF.

I hope one of the things you heard in the last few weeks is that you are not responsible for being anything more than what I am: a daughter who wants to be with her Father.

We can spend our lives complicating God and criticizing things we aren't sure we agree with, but this truth will remain regardless: what He desires is our imperfect, questioning, broken, seeking, confused, and desperate hearts.

You may have noticed that there were a lot of facts in this Bible study, but there were also a lot of gaps. It isn't because I didn't do my homework; it's because I did.

Jesus never told us that if we don't love Him perfectly, we must not love Him at all.

Hear me say: I'm right beside you in trying to figure out how to embrace a human understanding of Jesus while still leaving room for the mystery that He intended to be exactly that—hidden in places we can't reach.

You'll never know how many times I prayed for you or how many times you actually strengthened my faith. I imagined that you and I were walking side-by-side. I don't see myself as the one at the chalkboard. I think we're two girls trying to help one another get closer to our Teacher.

I love you from afar, and I'm for you as a sister in Christ. One day—either here or there—I'll get to tell you that in person.

And yes, Janet. That includes you.

# GROUP SESSION GUIDE

## SESSION 8: REVIEW WEEK 7 HOMEWORK

* *What new things did you grasp from the Scripture this week in your homework?*

* *Day 1: Two Pharisees, Joseph and Nicodemus, took Jesus off the cross and buried Him. Evidently, they had become secret followers of Jesus at some point in time. Why do you think they chose this time to reveal their secret?*

* *Are you sometimes more of a secret follower of Jesus rather than a bold one? Explain.*

* *Day 2: The first person Jesus appeared to after He was resurrected was Mary Magdalene, a woman. Why is that appearance so significant?*

* *Paul stated in 1 Corinthians 15 that if Christ had not been raised, our faith is worthless. Why is the resurrection so vital to our faith?*

* *Day 3: Luke 24:27 says that Jesus started with Moses and all the prophets to tell the Emmaus road followers about Himself. Why did He start there? How would you use the Old Testament to tell someone about Jesus?*

* *Day 4: Jesus restored both the doubter, Thomas, and the denier, Peter. How have you experienced the loving forgiveness and restoration of Jesus?*

＊Day 5: If you're a believer, then you have the Holy Spirit of God living inside of you. You're now the temple. How do you currently see the Holy Spirit working in your life?

＊Jesus said He would return one day to get us. What are we supposed to be doing in the meantime?

**WATCH SESSION 8 (VIDEO RUN TIME: 8:09)**

## DISCUSS

＊What part of the video spoke to you the most? Why?

＊Angie says "I feel like I started breathing easier in my faith when I fully accepted that there isn't a formula." What does she mean by that statement? How can making our faith a formula hinder our relationship with Jesus?

＊How is faith a process? What has that process looked like in your life, doubts and all?

＊Are there days in your walk with Jesus when you don't feel that He is near? How do you continue to trust Him during those times?

＊You're having lunch with your neighbor or coworker who you know is not a Christian. She pauses in the conversation, looks right at you and asks, "Who is Jesus?" How do you answer?

Video sessions available for purchase or rent at *LifeWay.com/Matchless*

# ENDNOTES

## INTRODUCTION

1. C. S. Lewis, *Mere Christianity* (New York: HarperCollins, 1980), 53.

## WEEK 1

1. "Prophecy," *Holman Illustrated Bible Dictionary, Revised and Expanded* (Nashville, TN: B&H Publishing Group, 2015), 1303.

2. MJL, "Bar and Bat Mitzvah 101." My Jewish Learning. myjewishlearning.com. (retrieved April 17, 2020).

3. "Birthright," *Ultimate Bible Dictionary* (Nashville, TN: Holman Bible Publishers, 2019), 58.

4. Orr, James, M.A., D.D., General Editor, "Entry for 'LEAH.'" *International Standard Bible Encyclopedia* (1915). Accessed from biblestudytools.com/dictionsary/leah.

5. See this commentary for an explanation of the questions behind what made Joseph's coat special: Kenneth A. Mathews, *New American Commentary, Vol 01B: Genesis 11:27–50:26* (B&H Publishing Group, 2012).

6. "Cubit," *Holman Illustrated Bible Dictionary, Revised and Expanded* (Nashville, TN: B&H Publishing Group, 2015). Retrieved from https://app.wordsearchbible.com.

7. *Ultimate Bible Dictionary*, 95.

8. Jack Wellman, "What does the number forty (40) mean or represent in the Bible?," *Patheos*.com, posted on October 3, 2014.

## WEEK 2

1. John F. MacArthur, *MacArthur Study Bible* (Nashville: Thomas Nelson), 1421.

2. Max Anders and Rodney Cooper, *Holman New Testament Commentary, Vol. 02: Mark* (Nashville, TN: B&H Publishing Group, 2012). Retrieved from app.wordsearchbible.com.

3. "Rabbi," *Holman Bible Dictionary*, Trent C. Butler, ed. (Nashville, TN: Holman Bible Publishers, 1991), 1162.

4. Robert H. Stein, *New American Commentary Vol 24: Luke* (Nashville, TN: B&H Publishing Group, 2012). Retrieved from https://app.wordsearchbible.com.

5. *Ultimate Bible Dictionary*, 283.

6. Leon Morris, *Tyndale Commentaries: Luke* (InterVarsity Academic, 2015), 100.

7. Robert H. Stein, *New American Commentary, Vol 24: Luke* (Nashville, TN: B&H Publishing Group, 2012). Retrieved from https://app.wordsearchbible.com.

8. "Shepherd," *Holman Bible Dictionary*, Studylight.org. Accessed May 4, 2020.

9. Morris, *Tyndale Commentaries*, 101.

10. Leon Morris, as quoted in David Guzik, "Luke 2:9-14," Luke: Enduring Word Commentary, (Enduring Word Media (2016), 54.

11. *MacArthur Study Bible*, 1515.

12. Craig Blomberg, *New American Commentary Vol 22: Matthew* (Nashville, TN: B&H Publishing Group, 2012). Retrieved from https://app.wordsearchbible.com

## WEEK 3

1. Wellman, "What does the number forty (40) mean or represent in the Bible?"

2. Christopher Hodgkins, *Literary Study of the Bible: An Introduction* (Hoboken, NJ: John Wiley & Sons, Ltd, 2020), 354.

3. Hodgkins, 354.

4. Zondervan Academic, "Who was Herod?" BibleGateway Blog, December 19, 2017. Available at www.biblegateway.com.

5. Dr. Henrietta C. Mears, *What the Bible Is All About KJV: Bible Handbook* (Carol Stream, IL: Tyndale House Publishers, 2015).

6. "American 'Millennials' are Spiritually Diverse," LifeWay Research. Retrieved from https://lifewayresearch.com.

7. Stuart K. Weber, *Holman New Testament Commentary: Matthew* (Nashville, TN: B&H, 2000). Retrieved from https://app.wordsearchbible.com on March 24, 2020.

8. "10. Eyewitness Testimony in Luke's Gospel," Bible.org. Accessed April 23, 2020. Available online at https://bible.org/seriespage/10-eyewitness-testimony-luke-s-gospel.

9. "10. Eyewitness Testimony in Mark's Gospel," Bible.org.

10. *Ultimate Bible Dictionary,* 171.

11. "10. Eyewitness Testimony in Luke's Gospel," Bible.org.

12. "The Gospel of Mark," Blue Letter Bible https://www.blueletterbible.org/study/intros/mark.cfm. Accessed on March 24, 2020.

13. Craig L. Blomberg, *The New American Commentary—Matthew, Volume 22* (Nashville: TN, Broadman Press, 1992). Retrieved from https://app.wordsearchbible.com on March 24, 2020.

14. "Quotations from the Old Testament in the New Testament," Blue Letter Bible. Accessed April 23, 2020. Available from www.blueletterbible.org.

15. H. I. Hester, *The Heart of the New Testament* (Nashville, TN: Broadman Press, 1950).

16. Trent C. Butler, *Holman New Testament Commentary: Luke* (Nashville, TN: Broadman & Holman, 2000).

17. Matthew Henry, *The New Matthew Henry Commentary* (Grand Rapids, MI: Zondervan, 2010).

18. Robert H. Stein, *New American Commentary Vol 24: Luke* (Nashville, TN: B&H Publishing Group, 2012). Retrieved from https://app.wordsearchbible.com.

19. "Choose Your Own Adventure," Goodreads, Inc. Retrieved from www.goodreads.com/genres/choose-your-own-adventure.

20. "The 100 Most Read Bible Verses at Bible Gateway," Bible Gateway. Retrieved online from www.biblegateway.com/blog/2009/05/the-100-most-read-bible-verses-at-biblegatewaycom.


WEEK 4

1. Paul Enns, *Living the New Testament: Daily Readings from Matthew to Revelation* (Grand Rapids, MI: Kregel Publications, 2010).

2. Enns, *Living the New Testament: Daily Readings from Matthew to Revelation.*

3. W.O.E. Oesterley, *Judaism and Christianity* (New York: The MacMillan Company, 1937).

4. Alfred Edersheim, *The Life and Times of Jesus the Messiah, Volume 11* (New York: Longmans, Green, and Co., 1900).

5. Philip W. Struble, *Zebedee and Sons Fishing Co.: Business Advice from the Bible* (Bloomington, IN: Westbow Press, 2017).

6. Jamie Snyder, *Real: Becoming a 24/7 Follower of Jesus* (Bloomington, MN: Bethany House Publishers, 2013).

7. Gerald L. Borchert, *New American Commentary, Vol 25A: John 1-11* (Nashville, TN: B&H Publishing Group, 2012). Retrieved from https://app.wordsearchbible.com. Accessed March 28, 2020.

8. Anders and Cooper, *Holman New Testament Commentary, Vol. 02: Mark.* Retrieved from app.wordsearchbible.com.

9. R. T. France Tyndale *New Testament Commentaries, Volume 1–Matthew: An Introduction and Commentary* (Downers Grove, IL: InterVarsity Press, 1985), 332. Retrieved from https://app.wordsearchbible.com on March 25, 2020.

10. *Ultimate Bible Dictionary,* 370.

11. *Ultimate Bible Dictionary,* 72.


WEEK 5

1. "Miracles, Signs, Wonders," *Holman Bible Dictionary,* 973.

2. "Christ, Son of David," James A. Brooks, *New American Commentary Vol 23: Mark* (Nashville, TN: B&H Publishing Group, 2012). Retrieved from https://app.wordsearchbible.lifeway.com.

3. "Mikvah," *Encyclopaedia Britannica.* Retrieved from www.britannica.com/topic/mikvah.

4. Max Anders and Kenneth O. Gangel, *Holman New Testament Commentary, Vol. 04: John* (Nashville, TN: B&H Publishing Group, 2012). Retrieved from https://app.wordsearchbible.com.

5. Matthew Henry, "Matthew Henry's Commentary on the Whole Bible (Complete), John," *Bible Study Tools.*

5. Matthew Henry, "Matthew Henry's Commentary on the Whole Bible (Complete), John," *Bible Study Tools*. Retrieved from www.biblestudytools.com. Accessed on April 30, 2020.

6. *Editors' note:* We're not really sure who said this. Some attribute it to Einstein, but others doubt its credibility.

7. *"Phobeō,"* Strong's G5399, Blue Letter Bible. Available online at www.blueletterbible. org. Accessed on May 5, 2020.

8. Brooks, *New American Commentary.* Retrieved online from https://app. wordsearchbible.com.

## WEEK 6

1. *Ultimate Bible Dictionary,* 203.

2. "11:7-8," Anders and Cooper, *Holman New Testament Commentary, Vol. 02: Mark.*

3. "Leaven," *Ultimate Bible Dictionary,* 271.

4. *"Diathēkē,"* Strong's G1242, Blue Letter Bible. Available online at www.blueletterbible. org.

5. "14:36," Anders and Cooper, *Holman New Testament Commentary, Vol. 02: Mark.*

6. "19:30," Anders and Gangel, *Holman New Testament Commentary, Vol. 04: John.*

7. MacArthur, *MacArthur Study Bible,* 1625.

8. Phlegon, quoted by Origen and Eusebius, found in Adam Clarke, *Adam Clarke's Commentary on the Bible* (Thomas Nelson Incorporated, 1997).

## WEEK 7

1. Anders and Cooper, *Holman New Testament Commentary, Vol. 02: Mark.* Retrieved from app.wordsearchbible.com.

2. Mary Jane Chaignot, "A Question about the Napkin Placed on Jesus Face," BibleWise. Available online at www.biblewise.com.

3. Tim Chester, "A Meal with Jesus," Christianity Today, June 17, 2011. Available online at www.christianitytoday.com.

4. John Piper, "Bethlehem: House of Bread," Desiring God. Available online at https:// www.desiringgod.org/articles/bethlehem -house-of-bread.

5. *"Metanoeo,"* Strong's G3340, Blue Letter Bible. Available online at www. blueletterbible.org. Accessed on May 5, 2020.

APPENDIX

# BECOMING A CHRISTIAN

In a few days, I will celebrate my twenty-year anniversary of the day that I accepted the Lord. That means I believed He was exactly who He said He was, and I repented for my sin and became a part of the body of Christ, also known as the bride of Christ.

Sometimes people call this the time when they were "saved" or "became a believer." And here's where I make a confession that will surely lead to a few more happy emails; I can't say I'm overly fond of the terminology. I don't know. I always think about the words I would use if I were sitting on a plane with someone who was curious about my faith, and I wouldn't use those words because they sound churchy. I'd answer them in a conversational way, not in a way that automatically made them feel outside of the story.

Jesus is coming back. He will rule the world, and all will be made right. Those of us who believe will be with Him for eternity in heaven, and those who don't will not.

This is without question the most important decision you will make in your life, and we started the study off with a sentence that leads to your answer: *Who do you think He is?*

If you have never accepted Christ as your Lord but would like to, pretend we're seat buddies on the plane (yes, I WILL share my pretzels) and read on to discover how you can become a Christian.

Romans 10:17 says, "So faith comes from what is heard, and what is heard comes through the message about Christ" (CSB).

I'll warn you; it isn't easy because our nature wants to run and hide from God. Thanks, Eve. The truth is, we're all sinners. We've all fallen short (Rom. 3:23).

But God loves you enough to offer you a new life with Him. In fact, He loves you so much that He died to rescue you from sin. Those aren't just words on a page—they're an invitation for you to believe and to be forgiven.

There aren't specific words, and there isn't a magic formula. It's the decision to tell God that you know there is nothing you can do to save yourself from sin, and you recognize that He is the only one who can.

It isn't enough to just be sorry about the fact that you've sinned; you have to genuinely repent for what you know to be true. We just can't do it on our own.

Talk to God.

Pray to Him.

Ask Him to reveal Himself to you, and when He does (and He will), bow your knee to Him and commit to spending the rest of your life as His disciple.

It's the most important decision you'll ever make, and if it's one you made here, I want to hear all about it.

In this very moment I am praying for you and asking the Lord to be so undeniable that you can't imagine a life without Him.

He wants nothing more, friend.

With love,

*Angie*